P · O · C · K · E · T · S

ANCIENT EGYPT

MUMMIFIED
HEAD

ANUBIS, THE JACKAL
GOD OF EMBALMING

FOOT CASE FROM
A MUMMY

OUTER AND INNER
MUMMY CASES

P · O · C · K · E · T · S

ANCIENT EGYPT

Written by
SCOTT STEEDMAN

GODDESS
HATHOR

LOTUS FLOWER
DRINKING CUP

SPHINX
SCULPTURE

DK

A DK PUBLISHING BOOK

Project editor Linda White
Art editor Ann Cannings
Assistant designer Kate Eagar
Senior editor Hazel Egerton
Senior art editor Jacquie Gulliver
Production Ruth Cobb
Editorial consultant Angela Thomas
Picture research Giselle Harvey
US editor Jill Hamilton
US consultant Stephen P. Harvey, Research Associate
University of Pennsylvania Museum

First American Edition, 1995
4 6 8 10 9 7 5 3
Published in the United States by
DK Publishing, Inc.,
95 Madison Avenue, New York, New York 10016

Copyright © Dorling Kindersley Ltd., London

Published in Great Britain by Dorling Kindersley Ltd.
Visit us on the World Wide Web at http://www.dk.com
Library of Congress Cataloging-in-Publication Data
Steedman, Scott
   Ancient Egypt / written by Scott Steedman, - - 1st American ed.
   p.   cm. - - (Pockets)
   Includes index.
   Summary: Surveys the history, culture, daily life, accomplishments, and religion of
the ancient Egyptians.
   ISBN 0-7894-0216-5
   1. Egypt - - Civilization - - To 332 B.C. - - Juvenile literature. 2. Egypt - -
Civilization - - 332 B.C.– 638 A.D.- -Juvenile literature. [1.Egypt - - Civilization - - To
332 B.C. 2. Egypt - - Civilization - - 332 B.C.–638 A.D. 3. Egypt - - Antiquities.] I. Title.
DT61.S865 1995
932 - - dc20   95-146
                                                            CIP

Color reproduction by Colourscan, Singapore
Printed and bound in Italy by L.E.G.O.

CONTENTS

How to use this book 8

INTRODUCTION TO ANCIENT EGYPT 10

Egypt today 12
The Nile 14
The sources 16
Before the pharaohs 18
The Old Kingdom 20
The Middle Kingdom 22
The New Kingdom 24

EGYPTIAN SOCIETY 26

The people of Egypt 28
Peasants and servants 30
Middle classes 32
The army 34
Egyptian women 36
The pharaoh 38
The royal house 40

LIFE IN ANCIENT EGYPT 42

Everyday life 44
Animals of the Nile 46
Farming 48
Food and drink 50
Trade 52
Egyptian housing 54
Clothing 58
Schooling and writing 62

GAMES AND LEISURE 66

Leisure pursuits 68
Playing games 70
Hunting and fishing 72
Banquets and feasts 74
Music and dance 76

BUILDING AND TECHNOLOGY 78

Skills and artistry 80
Boat-building 82
Weapons of war 84
The pyramids 86
Temples 90
Crafts 92
Egyptian art 94

RELIGION 98

Worship and beliefs 100
Myths and legends 102

The sun gods 104
Gods and goddesses 106
Magic and popular religion 108
Priests and rituals 110
Death and burial 112
Preparing a mummy 114
Journey to the afterlife 116
Mummy cases 118
Valley of the Kings 122

THE END OF AN ERA 126

Foreign pharaohs 128
The Greeks 130
The Romans 132

REFERENCE SECTION 134

Maps of Egypt 136
The dynasties 140
Famous pharaohs 142
Gods of ancient Egypt 146
Hieroglyphs 148
Architecture 150
Museums 152

Glossary 154
Index 156

HOW TO USE THIS BOOK

These pages show you how to use *Pockets: Ancient Egypt*.
The book is divided into a number of sections, which
cover different aspects of ancient Egyptian life. At the
back of the book is a useful reference section. Each new
section begins with a page that lists its contents.

EGYPTIAN LIFE
Ancient Egypt has been divided
into subject areas and arranged
in six main sections. In addition,
there is an introductory section,
which sets the scene by providing
you with an overview of the subject,
together with a brief history.

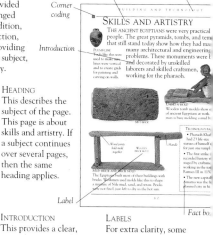

Heading   Running head

Corner
coding

Introduction

BUILDING AND TECHNOLOGY

SKILLS AND ARTISTRY

THE ANCIENT EGYPTIANS were very practical
people. The great pyramids, tombs, and tem[...]
that still stand today show how they had ma[...]
many architectural and engineering
problems. These monuments were [...]
and decorated by unskilled
laborers and skilled craftsmen,
working for the pharaoh.

PLUMB LINE
Tools like this were
used to make sure
lines were vertical
and to create grids
for painting and
carving on walls.

MUD BRICK

USING A MOLD
Wooden tomb models show w[...]
of ancient Egyptians at work. [...]
man is busy molding a mud br[...]

Wood joints
hold itself
together

Wooden
brick mold

Handle

MUD BRICK AND BRICK MOLD
The Egyptians built most of their buildings with
bricks. Workmen used molds like this to shape
a mixture of Nile mud, sand, and straw. Bricks
were not fired, just left to dry in the hot sun.

TECHNOLOGY FA[...]
• Pharaoh Khaf[...]
had 23 life-size
statues of himself [...]
for just one templ[...]
• The first strike [...]
recorded history w[...]
staged by craftsme[...]
working in the tom[...]
Ramses III in 115[...]
• The new capital [...]
Amarna was the fir[...]
of ... planned city in hi[...]

8 2

Fact bo.

CORNER CODING
The corners of
every page in the
main section are
color coded to
remind you which
section you are in.

■ EGYPTIAN SOCIETY

■ LIFE IN ANCIENT EGYPT

■ GAMES AND LEISURE

■ BUILDING AND
TECHNOLOGY

■ RELIGION

■ THE END OF AN ERA

HEADING
This describes the
subject of the page.
This page is about
skills and artistry. If
a subject continues
over several pages,
then the same
heading applies.

Label

INTRODUCTION
This provides a clear,
general overview of the
subject. After reading the
introduction, you should
have a good idea what
the pages are about.

LABELS
For extra clarity, some
pictures have labels. They
may give extra information,
or identify a picture when it
is not obvious from the text
what the picture actually is.

RUNNING HEADS

The running heads at the top of each page remind you which section you are in. The top of the left-hand page tells you the name of the section, and the top of the right-hand page tells you the subject of these two pages. The subject here is Skills and Artistry and it is in the Building and Technology section.

CAPTIONS AND ANNOTATIONS

Every illustration on a page has a caption. Each caption will go into a specific area of a subject. In addition to captions, there may also be annotations. These are in *italics* and draw your attention to particular features of an illustration. Annotations usually have leader lines.

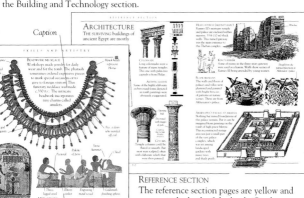

Caption

Annotation

FACT BOXES

The introductory pages to each section and subsection have fact boxes. These boxes contain interesting, at-a-glance information about the subject covered in that section.

REFERENCE SECTION

The reference section pages are yellow and appear at the back of the book. On these, you will find useful facts, dates, and charts. This section includes maps showing ancient sites, a list of dynasties, famous pharaohs, and a feature on reading and writing hieroglyphs.

GLOSSARY AND INDEX

There is a glossary and an index at the back of the book. The glossary defines and explains words and terms in this book that are specific to ancient Egyptian life. The index lists every subject alphabetically.

INTRODUCTION TO ANCIENT EGYPT

EGYPT TODAY 12
THE NILE 14
THE SOURCES 16
BEFORE THE PHARAOHS 18
THE OLD KINGDOM 20
THE MIDDLE KINGDOM 22
THE NEW KINGDOM 24

EGYPT TODAY

THE NILE RIVER and the Sahara Desert dominate Egypt. Until recently, the Nile flooded every year, bringing fertile black soil to the farmland on its banks. The ancient Egyptians called this lush strip the "black land," the land of life. The scorching desert was the "red land," the land of death.

CAIRO
Egypt's capital, Cairo, is the largest city in Africa, with a population of over 11 million. It was founded by Muslims in A.D. 969, more than a thousand years after the last pharaoh.

SAILING ON THE NILE
The Nile is the longest river in the world, flowing 4,145 miles (6,670 km) from the highlands of East Africa to the Mediterranean Sea.

FACTS ABOUT EGYPT
• The Sahara is the world's largest desert.

• Egypt is Africa's second biggest country (population: 55 million).

• Egypt has been a Muslim country since A.D. 642.

• The Aswan High Dam, built in 1969–70, ended the annual floods.

PYRAMIDS AND SPHINX
These famous monuments are both in Giza, on the outskirts of Cairo. They were built 4,500 years ago, during the period known as the Old Kingdom.

QUEEN HATSHEPSUT'S TEMPLE
Millions of tourists come to
Egypt every year to visit its great
monuments and museums. This
is Queen Hatshepsut's mortuary
temple at Deir el-Bahri on the
west bank of the Nile near Luxor.

KING'S COFFIN
The Egyptians had
elaborate beliefs
about life after
death. Pharaohs
and the elite were
mummified and
buried with a
wealth of treasure
in decorated
tombs. These
are a rich source
of information
on ancient life.

MODERN MAP WITH OLD SITES
Buildups of silt in the north
has altered Egypt's coastline.
Other changes are the Suez
Canal and Aswan Dam.

Mediterranean Sea

Suez
Canal

Alexandria

LIBYA

Bubastis
Giza · Heliopolis
Saqqara · · Cairo
Memphis

SINAI

Sahara
Desert

Hermopolis · Beni Hasan
· Amarna

EGYPT

Abydos · · Thebes
Valley of · Karnak
the Kings (Luxor)

Red
Sea

Aswan
· Lake Nasser
Abu Simbel · 1st cataract
2nd cataract

NUBIA

THE NILE

EGYPT HAS BEEN CALLED "the Gift of the Nile." All the water for drinking, bathing, and watering crops came from the great river. The Nile was also Egypt's main highway. The dominant wind blew from north to south, so boats could float downstream with the current or sail upstream against it.

ANCIENT WAYS
Egyptians still grow crops and raise livestock on the banks of the Nile, as they have been doing for more than 7,000 years.

Steering oar

Sun canopy

Steersman

TOMB MODEL FOR USE IN THE AFTERLIFE

Man rowing

FISHING NET

Prow

FISH HOOKS

BOAT
A text from c.1100 B.C. records "Merchants sail up and downstream, eager to convey goods from one place to another and to supply whatever is needed anywhere."

HUNTING AND FISHING
The Nile teemed with life. Men hunted birds in the marshes and caught fish with nets or hooks and lines. Crocodiles and hippos could be dangerous because they could overturn boats.

Protruding
ribs

Shrunken
stomach

Emaciated
limbs

OLD
KINGDOM
RELIEF
(c.2340 B.C.)

Mediterranean Sea

Ancient
coastline

LOWER
EGYPT

● Bubastis

● Heliopolis

● Memphis

Area of fertile
floodplain

Re—

● Amarna

● Abydos   ● Thebes

UPPER
EGYPT

FAMINE
Carvings like this show how a low
flood could cause crops to fail and
lead to starvation. High floods
had the same effect, because
the land was too slow to drain.

SAILING THE NILE
The hieroglyph
khenti, to travel
south, was a boat
with a sail; *khed*,
to travel north,
was a boat with
the sail down.

TRAVEL SOUTH

TRAVEL NORTH

PAPYRUS
This reed plant once flourished in
Egypt's river marshes. The ancient
Egyptians turned the pithy stem into a
kind of paper for writing and painting.

UPPER AND LOWER EGYPT
Ancient Egypt was divided into
Upper and Lower Egypt. North, or
Lower Egypt, is the Delta – a flat,
green area of marsh and grassland.
Upper Egypt, in the south, is a
steep river valley – a hot, dry land
where the desert is never far away.

THE SOURCES

OUR KNOWLEDGE of ancient Egypt comes from buildings, objects, and writings. Many disappeared over the centuries. Thieves stole treasures, and the desert sands invaded temples and tombs. But a hot, dry climate preserved monuments well. Egyptologists study these, and other sources, for clues to Egypt's past

MYSTERIOUS LAND
Sources can never give a complete picture of the past. This is the Queen of Punt, a land somewhere to the south. We still do not know exactly where.

GUTENBERG BIBLE
Jews and Christians learned about Egypt from the Old Testament of the Bible (the Jewish Torah). It tells the story of the Jews' exile in Egypt, where many worked as slaves for the pharaoh.

THE FIRST PRINTED BIBLE

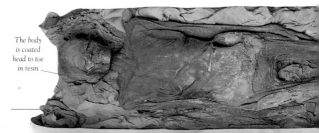

The body is coated head to toe in resin

Mummy case
Skeleton

NAPOLEON IN EGYPT
When the French general Napoleon invaded Egypt
in 1798, he brought a team of scholars and artists who
made detailed studies of temples, tombs, and mummies.
This sparked off the West's fascination with Egypt.

An owl stood for "m"   "Mouth" or "r"   Bandages

HIEROGLYPHS
Egyptian monuments, statues, and other artifacts are
covered in hieroglyphs, a type of picture-writing. In 1822,
French linguist Champollion discovered how to read
them and opened up a huge new source of information.

MUMMY SCAN
During the 19th century,
mummies were unwrapped,
often as public events.
This was destructive and
disrespectful. Now modern
scanners can create 3-D
X ray images of a mummy.

Linen
bandages

MUMMIFICATION
The Egyptians went to incredible lengths to
preserve their bodies for eternity. Mummies
give us all sorts of information about health, diet,
and disease. This woman's teeth were worn down
by a lifetime of chewing coarse bread. We can even
identify the plant oils used to preserve her skin.

BEFORE THE PHARAOHS

SETTLERS BEGAN TO FARM the Nile
Valley in about 5000 B.C. They
prospered and eventually formed
two kingdoms, Upper Egypt
and Lower Egypt. These early
Egyptians believed in life after
death. They buried their
dead in sand graves with
items for the next life.

NECKLACE
Sand graves have
revealed many items
of personal adornment,
such as jewelry of beads
and shells. This ancient
necklace is threaded
with semiprecious
stones from the
desert.

FLINT KNIFE
In this period, the Egyptians were already
skilled stoneworkers. They carved elegant
ceremonial knives and daggers. The flint blades
were set in handles made from
bone or ivory.

Carnelian

*Blade is
delicately
curved*

*Roofs
were
thatched*

*Wattle and
daub walls*

*Wood
beams above
doors and windows*

Toenail

MODEL HOUSE FROM GRAVE
The time before the pharaohs is known as the
Predynastic period (5000–3100 B.C.). In Upper
Egypt, farmers lived in small villages on the high
ground above the Nile, in houses like this.

FAIENCE BABOON
This is made from a glazed earthenware called faience, which first appeared in Egypt during this period.

Zigzag patterns on backs of hippos
Inlaid eyes

HIPPO BOWL
Early potters used Nile silt and clay. The river was also a source of inspiration. This bowl is decorated with hippos.

SHEEP SHAPE
This sheep-shaped stone palette was for grinding makeup. Others are in the form of hippos, turtles, and falcons. These mysterious objects probably had a magical purpose as well.

Dry skin

Hair

Bodies were buried facing west to the setting sun

Knees pulled up against chest

GINGERELLA
She died 5,000 years ago. But this Egyptian woman's hair, skin, and nails have been remarkably well preserved by the hot desert sands. She has been nicknamed Gingerella because of her red hair.

THE OLD KINGDOM

EGYPT WAS UNIFIED for the first time in about 3100 B.C., more than 400 years before the start of the Old Kingdom, or "Pyramid Age." Under the stable rule of powerful pharaohs, the country's economy and culture flourished. Art and architecture reached a peak with the building of the great pyramids at Giza.

DOUBLE CROWN
As a symbol of his power, the pharaoh wore the *pschent* or double crown. This combined the White Crown, worn by the kings of Upper Egypt, and the Red Crown of Lower Egypt's kings.

RULER OF TWO LANDS
The union of Egypt is shown here by the entwined lotus (symbol of Upper Egypt) and papyrus (Lower Egypt). One of the pharaoh's official titles was "Ruler of the Two Lands."

Painted limestone

Papyrus plant

Lotus

KING KHAFRA'S THRONE (DETAIL)

ROYAL COUPLE
These beautiful statues are Prince Rahotep and his wife Nofret. They were found near the pyramid of his father, King Sneferu. The statues are so lifelike it is hard to believe they are 4,600 years old. The eyes are rock crystal, with irises of purple amethyst.

FIRST PHARAOH?
Legend tells that
Egypt was united
by Menes, a king
from Upper Egypt
who conquered
the north. Experts
believe he may be
King Narmer (here
wearing the White
Crown). On the other
side of this palette, he
wears the Red Crown.

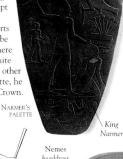

NARMER'S
PALETTE

King
Narmer

STEP PYRAMID
The first pyramid was built
at Saqqara for King Djoser in
c.2680 B.C. This huge stepped
structure is 198 ft (60 m) high.
Like most pyramids, it is a tomb.
Djoser and his family were
buried in chambers far beneath.

KHUFU
SMITES
ENEMY
CHIEF

MIGHTY KINGS
Kings Khufu, Khafra, and
Menkaura, builders of the
Pyramids of Giza, were
among the most powerful.
They must have directed
Egypt's entire economy
into building their tombs.

GOD-KING
The Egyptians believed
that the pharaoh was the
son of the sun god Ra. The
king was also associated with the
sky god, Horus, seen here as a
falcon protecting Khafra.

Nemes
headdress

Sky god,
Horus

Royal beard

THE MIDDLE KINGDOM

THE OLD KINGDOM COLLAPSED in about
2160 B.C., and Egypt was rocked by war
and chaos. It was eventually reunited by
Mentuhotep, who founded the Middle
Kingdom in 2040 B.C. Peace and
prosperity returned. Strong pharaohs
strengthened government and
foreign trade, and Egypt invaded
Libya and Nubia. Art revived,
and pyramids were built again.

SENUSRET I
This dynamic king took the throne
after sharing it for ten years with his
father, Amenemhat I. Senusret I fought
the Libyans and Nubians and built many
grand temples. The earliest known
literary texts were written in his court.

ETERNAL STONE
This noble died in abou
1850 B.C. Statues like
this were placed in loca
temples, so relatives did
not have to travel to a
tomb with offerings.

*Spells cover
coffin inside
and out*

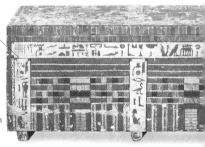

MUMMY CASE
Middle Kingdom coffins were
painted with magical spells to
help the soul on its journey
through the underworld to
the next life. During the Old
Kingdom, these spells – known
as the Pyramid texts – had
been carved in royal tombs.

AMENEMHAT III
During his long and peaceful reign (1854–1808 B.C.) this powerful pharaoh built temples, border forts, two pyramids, and undertook a land reclamation scheme.

BLACK PYRAMID
This is the first pyramid of Amenemhat III, which he built at Dahshur. Like all Middle Kingdom pyramids, the core is of mud bricks rather than stone. These have collapsed in a shapeless heap.

UNDER THE BLACK PYRAMID
Kings built mazes of false passages and hidden doors to try to conceal their burial chambers from robbers. It did not work. The Middle Kingdom collapsed in 1750 B.C., and all the pyramids were looted during the chaos that followed.

Pyramid enclosure wall

Extent of rubble

King's burial chamber

Entrance

False eyes allow mummy to "see" out

OSIRIS

GOD OF THE DEAD
The worship of Osiris, god of death and rebirth, spread across Egypt in the Middle Kingdom. He offered all Egyptians, not just those close to the pharaoh, the hope of an afterlife.

THE NEW KINGDOM

THE GREATEST PERIOD of Egypt's history was the New Kingdom (c.1550–1086 B.C.). Warrior kings, such as Ahmose I and Thutmose III, expanded the empire into Nubia, Libya, and the Middle East. Many temples were built, and pharaohs were buried in painted tombs in the Valley of the Kings.

WAR CROWN
The pharaoh's new image was as a war leader. He adopted the Blue Crown, or war helmet, and was seen as a living form of a warrior god.

UNFINISHED BUST OF AKHENATEN

RAMSES THE GREAT
In his 67 years on the throne, Ramses II built more monuments than any other pharaoh. This is the massive rock-cut temple of Abu Simbel. The four statues of Ramses II are each 65 ft (20 m) high.

AKHENATEN, HERETIC PHARAOH
Pharaoh Amenhotep IV introduced a new religion, the first in history based on the worship of one god (the Aten). He even changed his name to Akhenaten. After his death, his name was scorned, his city abandoned, and the gods were reinstated.

WAR CHARIOT
To expel Asian invaders,
the first pharaohs of
the New Kingdom built an
efficient army. This included corps of war
chariots, copied from the Asian enemy.

MASS GLASS
Factories, mass-producing
colorful glass vessels, were
set up near many palaces.
Glass was also cast to
decorate jewelry, furniture,
and even mummy cases.

TOMB OF SENNEDJEM (DEIR EL-MEDINA)
The Egyptians gave up on pyramid tombs, which were
too easy to find and rob. Instead, they were buried in
tombs cut deep into the rock in barren spots like the
Valley of the Kings and the Valley of the Queens.

TUTANKHAMUN'S SECOND COFFIN
The tombs in the Valley of the Kings were robbed long ago.
The only one found intact belonged to an obscure boy-king
called Tutankhamun. The glittering treasures
inside amazed the world.

Colored
glass

EGYPTIAN SOCIETY

THE PEOPLE OF EGYPT 28

PEASANTS AND SERVANTS 30

MIDDLE CLASSES 32

THE ARMY 34

EGYPTIAN WOMEN 36

THE PHARAOH 38

THE ROYAL HOUSE 40

THE PEOPLE OF EGYPT

AT THE TOP of Egyptian society was the pharaoh. He commanded the army and ruled the country through a network of nobles, officials, and scribes. Skillful craftsworkers were kept busy building and decorating temples and tombs. But most Egyptians were peasants who worked the land.

AT THE PHARAOH'S SIDE
In life as in death, the king was surrounded by his nobles. This noble's tomb is in the shadow of King Khufu's Pyramid.

Tomb of Seshemnofer

SERVANT GIRL
Many women worked as servants in the houses of the rich. This wooden palette is in the shape of a serving girl, carrying a large pot on one shoulder. It is a makeup container; the top slides open and closed.

A KEEPER OF RECORDS
Scribes were important because they were among the few who could read and write. They recorded many details of everyday life.

FACTS ABOUT PEOPLE

• A massive tomb recently discovered in the Valley of the Kings (1995) shows that it contains at least some of Ramses II's many sons.

• When the pharaoh praised one man's work, the man died of shock.

HARVEST SCENE
Farming life followed the seasons. As
soon as the summer's crop was ripe,
farmers rushed to harvest it before
the Nile flooded the land again.
These oxen are treading the grain.

OFFICIAL
he state was
ghly bureaucratic.
very town had
ficials. These civil
rvants collected
xes, regulated
usinesses, and
ganized loans and
arriage contracts.

CRAFTSMEN
Most craftsmen were employed
in workshops run by royal
palaces or temples. This
carpenter is building a
ship for a wealthy patron.

MUSICIAN
The Egyptians believed in
enjoying life. Dancers and
musicians performed at the royal
courts and at private dinner
parties. They also entertained
the bustling crowds during
festivals and celebrations.

KING AND CAPTIVE
The pharaoh was seen as a living god.
He led in battle and protected Egypt
from famine, disease, and chaos. This
is symbolized by this statue of pharaoh
Ramses IV gripping a captive enemy.

PEASANTS AND SERVANTS

THE VAST MAJORITY of ancient Egyptians were peasant farmers. They worked in the fields by the Nile, channeling the floodwaters and planting and harvesting crops. Many others worked as servants or laborers. Few of them could read or write. But they enjoyed more freedom than slaves, who were rare.

FOREIGN SLAVES
Slaves were never an important part of Egyptian society and were rare until the New Kingdom. Most slaves were foreigners, captured during Egypt's wars abroad. Here a scribe registers foreign captives

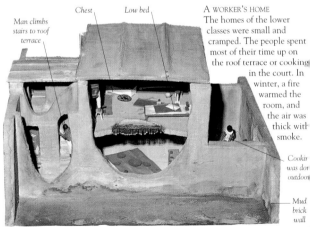

Chest

Low bed

Man climbs stairs to roof terrace

A WORKER'S HOME
The homes of the lower classes were small and cramped. The people spent most of their time up on the roof terrace or cooking in the court. In winter, a fire warmed the room, and the air was thick with smoke.

Cooking was done outdoors

Mud brick wall

A BEATING
Peasants who did not pay their taxes were beaten. More serious criminals were whipped or had their noses cut off and then were sent to mines in Sinai or Nubia.

GRAPE PICKING
Harvest time was very busy. These men are picking grapes and carrying them in buckets to the press. The squeezed juice was turned into wine.

TRAMPLED UNDER FOOT
These bound Libyans, painted on the soles of shoes, symbolized Egypt's power over foreigners. Slaves could be bought and sold like cattle, but they could also rent land and earn their freedom.

SERVANT GIRL
Most domestic servants were just poor. But some were female slaves who had escaped debt by selling themselves into slavery. The purchaser agreed to protect and feed the slave – and might later free her.

WOODEN MODEL
OF SERVANT
GRINDING
GRAIN

Quern
(grind
stone)

MODEL WORKER
Egyptians believed that, in heaven, they would work for the gods in the *Field of Reeds*. The rich were buried with model *shabti* figures, to do the hard work for them.

MIDDLE CLASSES

EGYPT'S EFFICIENT administration
was run by an educated middle
class of scribes and officials. Military
officers ran the army, while priests
organized prayers and offerings in the
temples. Lower on the social pyramid
were craftsworkers and traders – but
they still had a much better standard
of living than the peasant farmers.

ARTISANS
Jewelers present finished
works to their workshop
supervisor. Craftsmen
worked long hours in
hot, dirty conditions and
were given little persona
credit for the beautiful
works of art they produce

MEDICAL DOCTOR
This is one of just two known images
of a doctor at work. Many priests
and scribes were also doctors. Some
specialized in treating the eyes, teeth,
or the head. One priest had the
title "Doctor to the King's Belly."

A variety
of trees

Sistrum
(ceremonial rattle)

Incense
cone

The garden pool
would have
been stocked
with fish

PRIEST

In countless temples throughout the land, teams of priests and priestesses made offerings to the gods in the name of their pharaoh. In return, they were rewarded with land and a generous income.

Shrine of god Atum

SERVANT

Affluent middle-class families had servants to cook, clean, and help them wash and dress. This servant is placing an incense cone on his master's head, ready for a night out.

This official carries a wooden staff, which was a symbol of authority

Papyrus

SCRIBE

In most towns and villages, the only people who could read and write were scribes, which made them powerful and influential people. Art often shows them sitting cross-legged. This scribe is Pes-shu-per, c. 700 B.C.

Vents to catch cool breeze

WELL-TO-DO COUPLE

This detail from a papyrus shows the scribe Nakhte and his wife in the garden of their villa. A platform protects the house from high floodwaters. The couple are wearing elaborately pleated clothes and heavy wigs.

OFFICIAL

The government was run by state officials, ranging from the *Vizier*, the top statesman, to local officials who ran the day-to-day affairs in each district, or *nome*.

33

THE ARMY

EGYPT'S FIGHTING forces evolved from the Old Kingdom tradition of mustering troops when an emergency arose to the large, well-equipped army of the New Kingdom. In supreme control was the pharaoh. Below him, ranking officers commanded corps of soldiers, who fought on foot or in chariots.

WAR GALLEY
Armed with axes and bows, the navy fought sea battles from ships. These had figureheads of gods and names like "Wild Bull," "Star of Egypt," or "Soul of the Gods."

STING OF BATTLE
The pharaoh thanked soldiers for bravery in battle by giving them gold flies, made in the royal workshops by the best jewelers. Worn around the neck, the fly meant that a soldier had "stung" the enemy.

BATTLE FORMATION
In the periods of disorder that followed the Old Kingdom's collapse, many regional princes owned armies. This model, c.2000 B.C., from the tomb of Prince Mesehti may represent his private army.

STANDARD TACTICS
The pharaoh and his council of war planned the strategy. Every unit of the Egyptian army carried a standard so that they were easy to identify on the field of battle. Orders were given by war trumpet.

PEACE WORK
In peacetime, the army was
put to work digging ditches,
mining, or hauling stone
for temples and pyramids.
The navy went on trading
expeditions. This wall carving
from Queen Hatshepsut's temple
shows a trip, c.1496 B.C., to the
Land of Punt. The fleet returned
with baboons and incense trees.

Domed
houses
on stilts

Many different
trees and
plants

BORDER FORT
During the Middle Kingdom, massive mud-brick
forts were built to protect Egypt's border with Nubia.
Egyptian art never shows these forts under siege.

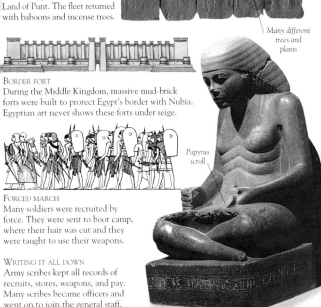

Papyrus
scroll

FORCED MARCH
Many soldiers were recruited by
force. They were sent to boot camp,
where their hair was cut and they
were taught to use their weapons.

WRITING IT ALL DOWN
Army scribes kept all records of
recruits, stores, weapons, and pay.
Many scribes became officers and
went on to join the general staff,
where battle tactics were decided.

EGYPTIAN WOMEN

WOMEN HAD CLEARLY DEFINED roles. They were responsible for looking after the house and bringing up the children. Many did a lot of back-breaking labor, such as working in the fields. But, by law, women had the same rights as men. A wife could even take her husband to court if he treated her badly.

A DELAYED BEATING
Egyptian criminals were beaten. But an exception was made with pregnant women, so as not to hurt the innocent unborn child. Punishment had to wait until after the birth.

Coffins fit inside each other

BRINGING UP BABY
A woman's main job was raising children. Mothers carried babies in slings. If a wife did not bear a son, her husband would take a mistress, and the family would adopt the child.

GOLDEN PRIESTESS
"Priestess" was one of the few titles women could have. Another was "Player of Music in the Temple." These golden coffins belong to Henutmehit, a priestess of the city of Thebes, c.1250 B.C.

NEFERTITI
This statue of the beloved wife of king Akhenaten was found in a sculptor's workshop in Amarna. After her husband's death Nefertiti may even have ruled on her own under a false name.

MARRIED COUPLE
This happy-looking couple are Katep and his wife Hetepheres, *c.*2500 B.C. Some unions were arranged, but other Egyptians married for love. Men could have several wives, but the marriage contract protected the wife and children, so most men could only afford one.

Woman's pale skin suggests she stayed in the home

BREAST MILK JUG
Mothers breastfed their babies openly. One carving even shows Queen Nefertiti nursing her daughter. Excess milk may have been kept in jugs like this. Mothers with a short supply prayed to the goddess Isis.

Woman carries basket on head

Face of Hatshepsut

Base fitted in stand

Ceremonial beard

A WOMAN KING
Hatshepsut was the first woman to become a true pharaoh (1479–1457 B.C.). Like other pharaohs, Hatshepsut had herself portrayed as a sphinx.

WOMAN'S WORK
Many women were household servants. Others worked as wet nurses, bakers, weavers, singers, dancers, musicians, and even doctors. But women never held public office.

THE PHARAOH

EGYPTIANS BELIEVED their pharaoh was a living god. He alone could unite the country and maintain the cosmic order, or *Ma'at*. They believed that, when he died, he would achieve eternal life – not just for himself, but also for his people. The pharaoh's power was absolute. He led the army, set taxes, judged criminals, and controlled the temples.

HORUS
The pharaoh was associated with the gods of the sun and sky, especially the falcon-headed sky god Horus.

ROYAL NAME
A pharaoh's name was written inside a cartouche. This oval loop symbolized the king's power over "all that the sun encircles."

KING OF THE NILE
Hapy was the god of the Nile flood. He was portrayed as a king, wearing the royal *nemes* headdress and false beard. The woman's breasts were symbolic of his waters, which gave life to Egypt.

Thutmose IV

ANKH

The ankh was the symbol of life. In art, only gods or kings carry this symbol. Many paintings show a god or goddess giving life to a pharaoh by touching his mouth with the ankh.

SYMBOLS OF THE PHARAOH

Tutankhamun carries a crook and flail and wears the striped *nemes* headcloth and ceremonial beard. The vulture and cobra on his brow represent Upper and Lower Egypt, respectively.

The Uraeus (said to spit fire at the king's enemies)

Vulture goddess Nekhbet

Nemes headcloth

PEPY II

This pharaoh ruled for 94 years. Every 30 years the pharaoh was recrowned in the *Sed* festival, a jubilee celebration. The highlight was a race in which the king ran a course to prove his fitness to rule.

False beard

Crook

OSTRICH-FEATHER FAN

The pharaoh was almighty. Servants fanned him, and visitors kissed the ground before him. But anyone who tried to touch him without permission risked death.

THE ROYAL HOUSE

IMPORTANT OFFICIALS were called "Friends of the Pharaoh." They had titles like "Fanbearer on the Right of the King" and "Master of the Horse." Many of them lived at the palace. On great state occasions, they would be joined by high priests and officials from all over Egypt.

ROYAL SPORT
The sport of kings and their courts was hunting. Noblemen killed birds with throwing sticks. The cartouche of pharaoh Akhenaten is painted on this fragile example, which was probably only ever used for ceremonial purposes.

RAMSES III AND HAREM
The pharaoh lived in a harem, a court of many wives and other women. They washed and dressed him many times a day and catered to his every need.

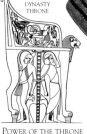

18TH DYNASTY THRONE

POWER OF THE THRONE
The pharaoh's might was visible throughout the palace. This throne has bound captives under the seat, showing the king's control over foreigners and his role as defender of Egypt.

TUTANKHAMUN'S OFFICIALS
A painting in Tutankhamun's tomb shows the court officials dragging the king's coffin at his funeral. In his lifetime, they would have helped the king in the day-to-day affairs of state.

PREGNANT QUEEN
This is the only known image of a pregnant queen. She is the mother of King Thutmose III. One king could have many wives. To keep the dynastic line pure, pharaohs often married their sisters and cousins – and sometimes even their own daughters.

A PRINCE
It was very important for the pharaoh to have an heir. If his chief wife had no sons, a boy born by one of his other wives became heir. If he had no sons, the next pharaoh could start a new dynasty.

RAMESSIDE QUEEN

COURT OFFICIAL
This is Sennefer and his wife. He was "Prince of the Southern City" (Thebes) and "Administrator of Granaries" in c.1400 B.C. Sennefer's wife was a royal wet-nurse.

GODDESS QUEEN
The pharaoh's chief wife ruled beside him as his queen. She was also looked upon as a god on earth. The king represented the all-powerful sun god, while she was associated with Hathor, goddess of love, and Isis, the mother goddess.

LIFE IN
ANCIENT EGYPT

EVERYDAY LIFE 44
ANIMALS OF THE NILE 46
FARMING 48
FOOD AND DRINK 50
TRADE 52
EGYPTIAN HOUSING 54
CLOTHING 58
SCHOOLING AND WRITING 62

EVERYDAY LIFE

EGYPTIAN LIFE revolved around three seasons. During the flood, *akhet* (July to October), farm work stopped. *Peret*, the time of plowing and sowing, began when the waters went down in November. The busiest season was *shemu*, the harvest. From March to June, farmers worked hard to bring in the crops before the river rose again.

IRRIGATION DEVICE
Farmers used *shadufs* to raise water from the river. They irrigated the land by using a system of canals and dikes.

PYRAMID
Thousands of farmers had nothing to do during the flood season. So they joined the pharaoh's skilled labour force to work on huge building projects like temples or pyramids. This is the remains of the Meidum pyramid, built around 2550 B.C. for the pharaoh Sneferu.

Limestone core of pyramid

Farmland on edge of desert

HUNTING IN THE MARSHES
Work and play centered on the Nile. This tomb carving shows cattle being herded across the river. The calf being helped into a boat is about to be grabbed by a crocodile.

In the Old Kingdom, silver was far rarer than gold

THE SIDELOCK OF YOUTH
Children often ran around naked in the hot climate. They are usually shown with a distinctive hairstyle.

RINGS
Both men and women enjoyed wearing jewelry, which was often made from precious metals. These seal rings have scarabs on one side and good-luck designs engraved on the other side.

CATTLE COUNT
This wooden model shows the cattle count, an event that took place every year or so. This was a means of assessing a person's wealth. The cattle are driven past scribes, who write down the numbers for the owner's tax records.

ANIMALS OF THE NILE

IN ANCIENT TIMES, a great variety of animals thrived in Egypt. The desert was home to lions, wolves, antelopes, wild bulls, and hares. The river marshes echoed with the loud cries of exotic birds. Crocodiles lazed on the banks, while hippos wallowed in the water. At night, owls, jackals, and hyenas came out in search of food.

CAT MUMMY
Sacred to the goddess Bastet, cats were popular pets. Cats were often mummified and buried in cat-shaped coffins after they died.

CROCODILE GOD
Many people were killed by the huge Nile crocodiles. The animal was worshipped as the god Sobek

ANIMAL GAMES
This comical papyrus gives us a glimpse of ancient Egyptian humor. Like the lion and antelope playing senet, the animals are all doing things that are wildly out of character.

Senet was a popular board game

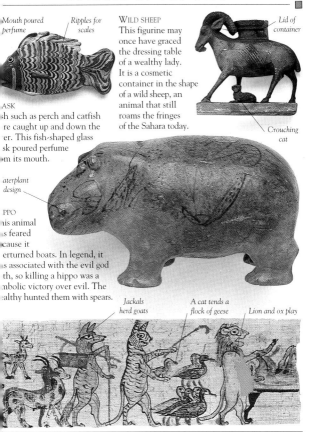

Mouth poured perfume

Ripples for scales

ASK
h such as perch and catfish
re caught up and down the
er. This fish-shaped glass
sk poured perfume
m its mouth.

WILD SHEEP
This figurine may
once have graced
the dressing table
of a wealthy lady.
It is a cosmetic
container in the shape
of a wild sheep, an
animal that still
roams the fringes
of the Sahara today.

Lid of container

Crouching cat

aterplant design

PPO
his animal
s feared
cause it
erturned boats. In legend, it
s associated with the evil god
th, so killing a hippo was a
nbolic victory over evil. The
althy hunted them with spears.

Jackals herd goats

A cat tends a flock of geese

Lion and ox play

4 7

FARMING

EGYPTIAN LIFE was based on farming t[h]e rich flood plain of the Nile. The ma[in] crops were emmer wheat, barley, and flax. Farmers also grew beans, lentils, onions, leeks, cucumbers, and lettuce in garden plots, and fruits like grapes, dates, figs, and pomegranates. Animal[s] raised for meat included cattle, pigs, sheep, goats, geese, and ducks.

PICKING FIGS
Ancient Egyptians loved sycamore fruits. So did baboons, which were trained to climb the trees and pick the fruit.

Scribes making tax records

Wooden chest

Tomb owner

Man with [jar] of water

Man drinking water from jar

Mother with baby

Workers cutting grain with sickles

Men carry[ing] grain in ba[skets]

4 8

PLOWING THE FIELDS

his wooden tomb model shows a man
lowing. The wooden plow is being
ulled by two oxen. The plowman
sed a hoe if he needed to break up any
eavy clumps of soil. Another man would
have followed behind, sowing seed.

Man guides
plow

The wooden blade
cuts through
the soil

WATERING THE CROPS

A network of dikes, pools,
and irrigation channels
crisscrossed the farmland.
Here, a man is carrying
buckets of water hung on
a yoke across his
shoulders.

Workers winnowing

HARVESTING GRAIN

This is a harvesting scene from a tomb.
Below, workers cut the grain and load it
into baskets. Above, other workers are
winnowing – throwing the grain into
the air to separate it from the chaff.
Scribes record
the quantity.

Protective
headcloth

LENTILS

WHEAT

DATES

Girls
squabbling

Linen
kilt

CROPS

The fertile
soil by the Nile
enabled Egyptian
farmers to grow a
large variety of crops.
Harvested grain was
stored in granaries and
used to make bread and beer.

FOOD AND DRINK

BREAD AND BEER were the two staples in an Egyptian's diet. Both were made in a similar way, using wheat or barley. Bakers also made a whole variety of cakes and pastries, often sweetened with dates or honey. There were many fruits and vegetables, but potatoes and citrus fruits were unknown. The wealthy enjoyed lavish banquets – feasting on meat, washed down with wine. Poor people were more likely to dine on fish and beer.

HONEY
Egyptians were the first people known to keep bees. Honey was collected to sweeten cakes, beer, and wine.

Wooden siphon

BEER STRAINER

Holes for straining

GRAPES

GRAPES AND WINE
Wall-paintings show workers picking grapes and squeezing them in a press. The wine matured in tall amphorae, inscribed with the year, type of grape, region, and vineyard owner.

WINEPRESS

BREWING BEER
Women made beer. They mixed bread dough with yeast and left it to ferment in large vats. A few weeks later, they filtered the mash. The mature beer was seasoned with spices or dates. It was very thick and had to be strained before drinking.

FOOD OFFERINGS
Egyptians brought food to temples and tombs to make sure the gods and spirits of the dead were well fed. This tomb carving shows bearers bringing a selection of offerings.

EVERYDAY FARE
Fruit, vegetables, and grain were grown in plenty. The Egyptians ate bread with every meal. Until the New Kingdom, when bakeries became common, most housewives made their own bread. Loaves came in many shapes, some made specially for religious rites such as offerings for the dead. This bread was placed in a tomb more than 3,000 years ago.

Baboons could not resist figs

MODERN FIGS

BREAD

MODERN DATES

AT THE BUTCHERS
This tomb model shows an ox being slaughtered. The meat would be roasted, boiled, or stewed. Rich Egyptians ate a lot of meat, which was often wild game from the hunt. Antelope, gazelle, porcupine, hare, and fowl such as quail and crane were all on the menu.

ANCIENT PALM TREE FRUIT

EGGS FOR THE PHARAOH
Ostrich plumes and eggs were often among the tributes sent to pharaohs from lands in the south.

TRADE

FOR MOST OF ITS HISTORY, ancient Egypt was the richest country in the world. The Egyptians grew more than enough food. So the surplus grain, along with linen, papyrus, and dried fish, was exported in exchange for luxury items such as incense, silver, and fine cedar wood. Horses came from Asia to the east, while, to the south, Nubia and Punt were a source of gold, ivory, ebony, and incense.

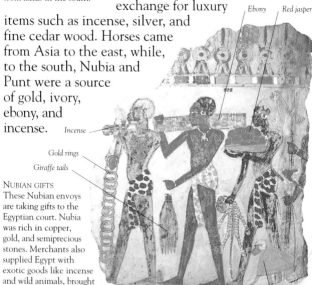

Ebony

Red jasper

Incense

Gold rings

Giraffe tails

NUBIAN GIFTS
These Nubian envoys are taking gifts to the Egyptian court. Nubia was rich in copper, gold, and semiprecious stones. Merchants also supplied Egypt with exotic goods like incense and wild animals, brought from lands farther south.

Live baboon

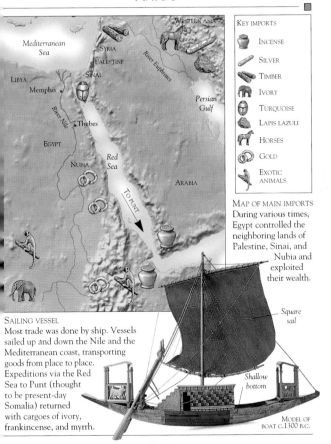

KEY IMPORTS

INCENSE

SILVER

TIMBER

IVORY

TURQUOISE

LAPIS LAZULI

HORSES

GOLD

EXOTIC ANIMALS

MAP OF MAIN IMPORTS
During various times, Egypt controlled the neighboring lands of Palestine, Sinai, and Nubia and exploited their wealth.

Square sail

SAILING VESSEL
Most trade was done by ship. Vessels sailed up and down the Nile and the Mediterranean coast, transporting goods from place to place. Expeditions via the Red Sea to Punt (thought to be present-day Somalia) returned with cargoes of ivory, frankincense, and myrrh.

Shallow bottom

MODEL OF BOAT C.1300 B.C.

EGYPTIAN HOUSING

EGYPTIAN HOMES were built to stay cool
From pharaoh's palace to worker's hut,
most houses were made from mud bricks
Many dwellings had roof terraces,
where people could take the air
in hot weather. Wealthy families
lived in large villas with lush gardens and fish-
stocked pools. In the cities,
the poorer people lived in
simple homes, crammed
together in a maze of alleys,
passageways, and squares.

MAKING BRICKS
Wet Nile mud was
mixed with sand and
straw, squeezed into
a wooden mold, and
then dried in the sun.

ANCIENT FRESCOES
The walls and ceilings of rich people's
houses were painted with colorful
designs, often composed
of geometric patterns and
plant motifs.

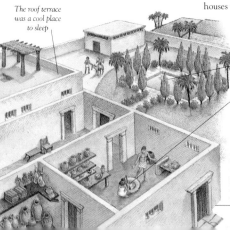

*The roof terrace
was a cool place
to sleep*

Decorative pond

*Kitchen area with
open fire for cooking*

INSIDE A HOUSE
In a typical house of a
well-off Egyptian, the
main living area was
placed some way from the
kitchen to avoid cooking
smells. Some bedrooms
had their own bathing
facilities and lavatories.

Flat roof

Chair

Stairs to upper story

Colonnaded entrance

Food was stored and cooked in courtyard

Bed

SIMPLE HOME

This pottery house (*c.*1900 B.C.) was placed in a tomb for the owner's use in the next life and shows architectural details that existed in houses of the period.

HOUSE FACTS

• Mud bricks were sometimes stamped with the name of the reigning pharaoh.

• A workman's week was nine days long – the 10th was a day of rest.

• Windows were small to keep out hot sunlight.

A VILLAGE ON THE NILE TODAY

Egyptian houses are still made of mud bricks. Some towns now sit on hills because they have been rebuilt again and again on the ruins of older settlements.

In the home

Egyptian houses were sparsely furnished.
Tables were rare, and many pictures show
people squatting cross-legged on the floor
rather than sitting on stools. Most people
slept on benches built into
the walls; only the wealthy
had real beds. The pieces of
furniture that have survived
have simple, elegant lines.
Many are exquisitely crafted,
with inlays of gemstones,
glass, and precious woods.

NOBLE CHAIRS
Only a wealthy Egyptian
household would have
chairs. Like tables, these
were usually low and wide
Legs were often carved to
look like lions' paws or
bulls' hooves.

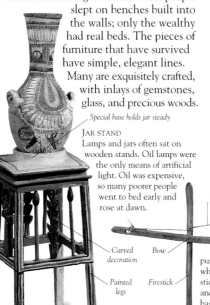

Special base holds jar steady

JAR STAND
Lamps and jars often sat on
wooden stands. Oil lamps were
the only means of artificial
light. Oil was expensive,
so many poorer people
went to bed early and
rose at dawn.

Carved decoration

Bow

Painted legs

Firestick

String

SERVANT
LOOKING
AFTER FIRE

Fanning flames

FIRE
This is the
only type of
Egyptian fire-
making device
found. A stick was
pushed into a wooden base,
while a bow looped around the
stick was moved quickly back
and forth. The friction set the
base on fire.

End of stick fits into groove

Base

Grooves blackened by fire

LION HEAD
Walls and furniture were decorated with images of gods, especially ones that protected the household. This lion head may represent Bes, a guardian of sleep, who is half lion, half dwarf.

Cup in shape of open lotus

Ducks

CONTAINERS
The first vessels, from over 7,000 years ago, were clay pots. Later, carved stone jars were produced. Faience, a colored and glazed earthenware, first appeared c.3200 B.C. This faience vase and cup from Thebes were made c.1450 B.C.

HEADRESTS
Instead of pillows, Egyptians slept on headrests. They were made from stone, wood, or bone. Much more comfortable than they look, headrests are still used in many parts of Africa.

Curved surface supports head

Wide base

String mesh netting

All six of Tutankhamun's beds have clawed feet

TUTANKHAMUN'S BED
Of the six beds discovered in Tutankhamun's tomb, this is the most spectacular. The carved ebony frame is completely covered in gold, and embossed panels are decorated with plant motifs. Another of his beds folded up for traveling.

CLOTHING

EGYPTIANS WORE simple linen clothes.
Men dressed in short kilts, leaving their
chests bare or draping a cloak or a strip
of linen over their shoulders. Women
wore long, tight-fitting dresses. On
cool evenings they might put on a
long-sleeved gown as well. In later
periods, tunics and dresses with
complicated pleats became
popular. Both women
and men wore wigs.

*Damp
cloth was
pressed
into
grooves*

PLEAT
BOARD

PRESSED PLEATS
Grooved boards like
this may have been used
to pleat the clothes of
well-to-do Egyptians.

COARSE LINEN
Ordinary Egyptians wore
coarse linen, while the rich
dressed in a lighter, finer
cloth. Finest of all was the
semitransparent "royal
linen." The Egyptians
knew about dyes,
but most linen was
left a natural white.

*Interwoven
flax fibers*

OFFICIAL ATTIRE
This is Mereruka, *vizier* to
King Teti in about 2340 B.C.
He is wearing the short kilt
typical of the Old Kingdom.
The kilt was tied at the waist,
often in an elaborate bow.

ROYAL DRESS

Egyptians were not prudish about their bodies. Kings are often shown in tiny kilts, and queens wore nearly transparent dresses. For important ceremonies, the king wore a long kilt and an elaborate cloak with countless pleats.

COURT LADY

Clothes were draped rather than cut to fit. The fringed, finely pleated dress of this noblewoman leaves one shoulder bare and reaches well below her ankles. Her heavy, braided wig is crowned with a circlet of flowers.

WEAVING LINEN

Women combed the stems of the flax plant to remove the spiky heads. Then they separated the fibers from the stalk and spun them on a spindle, weighted by a whorl. The spun threads were woven on a loom to make cloth.

Whorl

Flax
COMB

SPINDLE

Twine strap

DRESS FACTS

• Priests dressed statues of gods each morning and undressed them at night.

• Some peasants and fishermen worked naked.

• The wealthy used professional laundries. Poorer people did their washing in the river.

Rotating spindle twists fibers

SANDALS

Most Egyptians went barefoot. But priests and wealthy people wore sandals. These were made from leather or reeds like papyrus that flourished in the marshes by the Nile.

Jewelry and makeup

The Egyptians went to great lengths to look good. Men and women rubbed oil into their skins, painted their eyes with thick makeup, and sprinkled their clothes with sweet-smelling perfumes. At parties, women crowned their wigs with incense cones. These melted slowly, pouring scent onto their hair and clothes. The wealthy wore gold jewelry that sparkled with semiprecious stones.

Malachite

Galena

COLOR
Green eye paint came from malachite, black eye *kohl* from galena, and red for lips was made from iron oxide.

Iron oxide

EARRINGS

WIG FASHION
The Egyptians disliked body hair and shaved their heads and bodies with bronze razors. They wore wigs made from real human hair, curled or braided into many different shapes and styles.

Cowrie shell

Fish

Sidelock of youth

Heh, god of long life

Lotus flower

MAKEUP POT
Many makeup pots are works of art. This one is made from the rare blue stone anhydrite.

Gold trim

GOLDEN GIRDLE
This is part of a piece of jewelry that was worn around the waist. It is strung with colorful beads of carnelian, amethyst lapis lazuli, and turquoise, plus gold good-luck charms

COSMETIC PALETTE
This makeup container is carved and painted to look like a bunch of flowers. The buds are circles of ivory, dyed a soft pink. The swiveling top hides a hollow where cosmetic cream was stored.

Top swivels sideways

RACELET
obras protect the
y god Horus on
is bracelet made
r a prince.

Polished metal surface

Handle in shape of serving girl

Glass container with applicator

Lotus-style headdress

Duck   Leaves

METAL MIRROR
The Egyptians did not have glass mirrors. Instead, they admired their reflections in polished disks of copper or bronze. The bright, shining surfaces reminded the Egyptians of the sun they worshipped.

AKEUP FOR EYES
ohl was kept in pots and applied
th thin metal tools. Even
ildren wore kohl, which also
otected against eye infections.

SCHOOLING AND WRITING

MOST EGYPTIAN CHILDREN did not go to school. To be a goldsmith or a painter, a boy trained in a workshop or with a team of workers building a tomb. Scribes were given a more formal education, starting at age nine and lasting about five years. They had to study hard and were beaten if they were lazy. But it was worth it – scribes were among the only people who could read or write, and this gave them status.

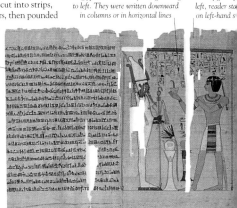

Layers placed at right angles

MAKING PAPYRUS
Paper was made from papyrus reed. The soft pith was cut into strips, placed in two layers, then pounded together to form a strong sheet.

Hieratic text always reads right to left

THREE SCRIPTS
Egyptian picture-writings are called hieroglyphs, the Greek word for "sacred carvings." Scribes later developed two other scripts, hieratic and demotic, which were much quicker to write.

Hieroglyphs read either left to right or right to left. They were written downward in columns or in horizontal lines

When figures f left, reader sta on left-hand s

WRITING TOOLS

A scribe often had to travel on official business or to make tax assessments on distant farms. He took a water pot with him and reed brushes, pens, and ink, which fitted into a wooden case. He mixed his own ink, making black from soot or charcoal and colors from ground-up minerals. Reed pens were first used in Egypt during the Greek period.

SCHOOLING FACTS

• Most sons followed their fathers' careers by training with them.

• Scribes made fun of other trades, saying such things as "a smith stinks more than fish roe."

• Girls received no formal training; few could read or write.

Reed is split to hold ink

Brush holder, water pot, and palette

HIEROGLYPH FOR "SCRIBE" OR "WRITING"

Case with inkwell and pens

Papyrus scroll

SEATED SCRIBE
This scribe is shown in the traditional seated position. The sculptor has given him a chubby stomach. This is common in ancient Egyptian art, because obesity was regarded as a sign of success.

Deciphering hieroglyphs

For nearly 1,500 years, no one could read hieroglyphs, the ancient Egyptian picture-writing. The French scholar Jean-François Champollion spent most of his life trying to break the code. He made his first breakthrough in 1822, while studying the Rosetta Stone, and soon experts were able to read the inscriptions that cover many Egyptian artifacts.

The text is a message of thanks to Pharaoh Ptolemy V

Demotic

The loop represents eternity

ROYAL NAMES
A pharaoh's name was written inside an oval loop called a cartouche. This piece of jewelry contains the cartouche of Senusret II.

Sa	Ankh	N	Ra	Nefer
Son	Life	Water	Day	Beautiful

PICTURES FOR WORDS AND SOUNDS
One hieroglyph can stand for either a word or a sound. For instance, a scribe would draw a goose both for the sound "sa" and the word "son."

A name of a pharaoh can be recognized because it is written within a cartouche

Hieroglyphs

JEAN-FRANÇOIS CHAMPOLLION (1790-1832)
A brilliant linguist, Champollion had mastered 12 languages by age 16. The first hieroglyphs he deciphered were pharaohs' names. By 1824, he had translated most of the symbols and begun to unravel Egyptian grammar.

"PTOLEMY" IN HIEROGLYPHS

"PTOLEMY" IN DEMOTIC

ΠΤΟΛΕΜΑΙΟΣ
"PTOLEMY" IN GREEK

THE ROSETTA STONE
Inscribed in 196 B.C., the Rosetta Stone was unearthed again in 1799. The text is repeated in hieroglyphs, demotic, and Greek. Champollion could read Greek, and so he used this text to translate the other two scripts.

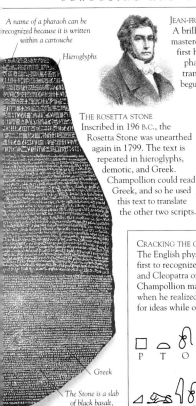

Greek

The Stone is a slab of black basalt, found near Rosetta in the delta

CRACKING THE CODE
The English physicist Thomas Young was the first to recognize the hieroglyphs for Ptolemy and Cleopatra on the Rosetta Stone. But Champollion made the great breakthrough when he realized that some symbols stood for ideas while others were simply sounds.

P   T   O   L   M   Y   S

K   L   E   O   P   A   T   R   A

GAMES AND LEISURE

LEISURE PURSUITS 68
PLAYING GAMES 70
HUNTING AND FISHING 72
BANQUETS AND FEASTS 74
MUSIC AND DANCE 76

LEISURE PURSUITS

THE EGYPTIANS LIVED LIFE to the full. At public festivals and private parties they feasted and drank, entertained by singers, dancers, and musicians. Children played out in the sunshine, while adults reveled in sports like hunting and fishing. In quieter moments they wrote poetry or enjoyed board games.

ANGLING
Egyptians were the first people to fish for pure pleasure. Nobles are often shown in armchairs, lazily dangling lines into their well-stocked garden pools.

ENTERTAINERS AT A BANQUET
Party scenes show how much the Egyptians liked music and dance. In this tomb painting, c.1400 B.C., one woman plays a double flute while others clap along or dance to the beat. In Egyptian art, it is very unusual to see faces front on.

LEISURE FACTS

• Egyptians swam backstroke and crawl. Upper-class children were given lessons.

• Farmworkers and fishermen had their own working songs.

• The world's first gaming piece was found in the grave of Pharaoh Den, c.2950 B.C.

STONE THROWER
This is the earliest known example of a sling. It dates from about 1900 B.C. and was found in the town of Kahun in the Faiyum Oasis. The sling was probably used to scare birds away from Kahun's vineyards and lush gardens. One end of the cord was looped around a finger to keep hold of the sling after firing.

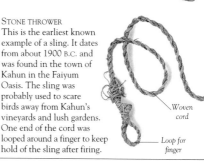

Woven cord

Loop for finger

FISHING IN THE MARSHES
These men are fishing from a reed boat. One man clubs the fish and puts them in a basket. Fish were sacred creatures in some areas and an important part of the diet in others. This even led to a war between neighboring towns.

Carved gazelle head

Plain stick

THROW STICKS
Dice did not reach Egypt until the Greek era. Before then, players threw sticks like these. Each stick has a flat and a rounded side. The number of flat sides facing up probably determined a player's move.

Carved sticks may have had different values from plain sticks

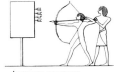

ARCHERY PRACTICE
Men hunted with bows and arrows. During the New Kingdom, archers shot at prey while riding chariots. They practiced archery by firing arrows at square targets made of copper. This drawing is copied from the Theban tomb of Min, a private man who taught archery to Amenhotep II.

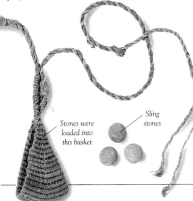

Stones were loaded into this basket

Sling stones

PLAYING GAMES

IN THE WARM EGYPTIAN CLIMATE, boys and girls spent a lot of time outdoors, swimming, dancing, riding donkeys, and enjoying games of leapfrog and tug-of-war. They played with balls, dolls, toy animals, and pets such as cats, birds, and monkeys. The most popular board game for adults was called senet. Tutankhamun liked it so much he was buried with four complete boards.

TOPS
Children spun these pottery tops with a twist of the fingers or a quick tug on a piece of string wrapped round the toy.

CLAY BALLS
Balls made of papyrus, cloth, and leather have all been found. These brightly painted clay balls were once filled with seeds or tiny lumps of clay to make them rattle when thrown.

String to move lower jaw

CAT TOY
Pulling the string on this carved wooden cat makes it open and close its mouth. Other ancient animal toys have glass eyes, movable legs and arms, and tails that wag.

CATCHING AND JUGGLING
This scene is copied from a Middle Kingdom tomb. These jugglers may have been professionals or people playing for fun or ritual.

HORSES AND MUMMIES

This wooden horse could be pulled along with a string through its nose. Nile mud animals, birds, and even tiny mummies lying in their coffins have been found. These may be toys made by children or votive offerings.

Senet

Wheel

Painted saddle

A GAME OF SENET

Senet was played by moving counters on a board of 30 squares – some were dangerous to land on, others were lucky. Unfortunately, the rules have been lost.

Fighting with wooden sticks

TOURNAMENTS

Men competed in games of boxing, wrestling, and fencing. King Ramses III held the first recorded fencing tournament in c.1250 B.C. Egyptian and allied soldiers fought with wooden sticks.

Winning position

Hieroglyph of pharaoh's name

SNAKE GAME

This was one of the earliest Egyptian board games. The playing surface is the shape of a coiled snake. Players started at the tip of the tail and tried to move balls toward the snake's head at the center.

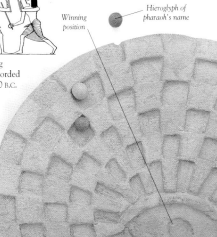

HUNTING AND FISHING

THE MAIN SPORT for well-to-do Egyptians was hunting. In early times, nobles stalked antelope, bulls, and lions on foot; later they hunted from horse-drawn chariots. Pharaohs were proud of their kills. Amenhotep III boasted of 102 lions in ten years as king, and Thutmose III claimed 120 elephants during one trip to Syria.

MAN WITH ANTELOPE
A man returns from the hunt. Trained dogs or even hyenas were used to catch antelope or to chase them into traps.

HUNTING WITH NETS
Marsh hunters netted both fish and wildfowl. They snared birds by baiting nets with grain or maggots.

FISHING FROM RAFTS
Egyptians fished for food and fun. During the Old Kingdom, fish were usually netted or speared. Later, angling became popular. The fishermen in this tomb relief are using hooks and nets to catch the fish.

Papyrus thicket

Throwing stick

Wife

Duck decoy

Daughter holds lotus

FOWLING
Nobles preferred to hunt birds with a throwing stick. It was like a boomerang and killed a bird by breaking its neck. This man has brought his family, including a pet cat, on the hunt.

HUNTING HYENAS
Hyenas got into game reserves and were killed along with animals kept there as quarry. They were also hunted as a menace to domestic flocks.

HIPPO HUNTING
These three men are spearing hippos from a papyrus raft. Spearheads were attached to long pieces of rope, so that the dying hippo could be hauled onto land.

BANQUETS AND FEASTS

EGYPTIANS HELD FEASTS to celebrate births, marriages, and religious festivals, or just to entertain friends. The wealthy enjoyed holding dinner parties. Cooks prepared a huge meal, flavored with imported herbs and spices. Dressed in their best clothes, guests sat on chairs or cushions on the floor, eating food with their fingers and drinking large quantities of wine.

LUTIST
Hosts hired musicians to play and sing at the feast.

Acrobat

AFTER-DINNER ENTERTAINMENT
Dinner parties were one of the main sources of employment for dancers, acrobats, and other entertainers. They performed after the meal was finished.

Wine amphorae

Food is piled high on tables

NEW KINGDOM BANQUET
This scene shows Egyptian hospitality at a dinner party. An army of servants ply the guests with food, wine, and presents.

TOO DRUNK TO WALK
Guests sometimes drank too much; some even vomited into bowls. These drunk men are being carried home from a party.

FOOD FOR THE FEAST
Pictures showing food offerings give us a good idea of the types of foods that wealthy hosts could serve their guests.

Scantily clad serving girl

Pleated clothes

Necklace presented as gift

Married couples sit arm in arm

Chair legs shaped like lions' paws

Incense cones

Servants offer wine and lotus flowers to guests

This group of women sitting together are probably unmarried

MUSIC AND DANCE

NO EGYPTIAN CELEBRATION would have been complete without music and dancing. At parties, singers performed to the music of harps, lutes, drums, flutes, and tambourines. Festival crowds chanted and clapped, carried along by the vibrant rhythm of Egyptian orchestras, while dancers leapt and twirled. Work, too, was often accompanied by music.

WOMAN PLAYING THE HARP
This model of a harpist was placed in a tomb to entertain guests at parties in the afterlife. In tomb pictures, harpists are often blind men.

SINGING ALONG
Singing played an important role in Egyptian music. These young women sing and dance, while beating tambourines and handheld drums.

Double crown of Egypt

CYMBALS
We do not know how Egyptian music sounded because it was never written down. The people played a wide range of instruments, suggesting that their music was varied. These bronze cymbals were used for rhythm and beat.

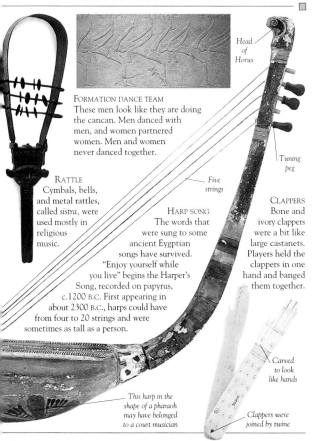

Head of Horus

FORMATION DANCE TEAM
These men look like they are doing the cancan. Men danced with men, and women partnered women. Men and women never danced together.

RATTLE
Cymbals, bells, and metal rattles, called *sistra*, were used mostly in religious music.

Five strings

Tuning peg

HARP SONG
The words that were sung to some ancient Eygptian songs have survived. "Enjoy yourself while you live" begins the Harper's Song, recorded on papyrus, c.1200 B.C. First appearing in about 2300 B.C., harps could have from four to 20 strings and were sometimes as tall as a person.

CLAPPERS
Bone and ivory clappers were a bit like large castanets. Players held the clappers in one hand and banged them together.

Carved to look like hands

This harp in the shape of a pharaoh may have belonged to a court musician

Clappers were joined by twine

BUILDING AND TECHNOLOGY

SKILLS AND ARTISTRY 80
BOAT-BUILDING 82
WEAPONS OF WAR 84
THE PYRAMIDS 86
TEMPLES 90
CRAFTS 92
EGYPTIAN ART 94

SKILLS AND ARTISTRY

THE ANCIENT EGYPTIANS were very practical people. The great pyramids, tombs, and temples that still stand today show how they had mastered many architectural and engineering problems. These monuments were built and decorated by unskilled laborers and skilled craftsmen, working for the pharaoh.

PLUMB LINE
Tools like this were used to make sure lines were vertical and to create grids for painting and carving on walls.

MUD BRICK

USING A MOLD
Wooden tomb models show scenes of ancient Egyptians at work. This man is busy molding a mud brick.

Wood joints hold mold together

WOODEN BRICK MOLD

Handle

MUD BRICK AND BRICK MOLD
The Egyptians built most of their buildings with bricks. Workmen used molds like this to shape a mixture of Nile mud, sand, and straw. Bricks were not fired, just left to dry in the hot sun.

TECHNOLOGY FACTS

• Pharaoh Khafra had 23 life-size statues of himself made for just one temple.

• The first strike in recorded history was staged by craftsmen working in the tomb of Ramses III in 1150 B.C.

• The new capital at Amarna was the first planned city in history.

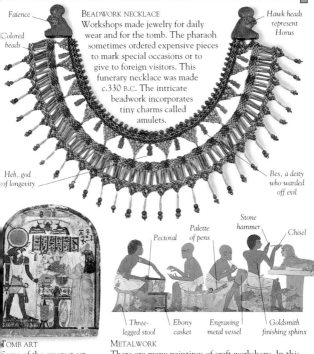

BEADWORK NECKLACE
Workshops made jewelry for daily wear and for the tomb. The pharaoh sometimes ordered expensive pieces to mark special occasions or to give to foreign visitors. This funerary necklace was made c.330 B.C. The intricate beadwork incorporates tiny charms called amulets.

Faience

Colored beads

Hawk heads represent Horus

Heh, god of longevity

Bes, a deity who warded off evil

Pectoral

Palette of pens

Stone hammer

Chisel

Three-legged stool

Ebony casket

Engraving metal vessel

Goldsmith finishing sphinx

TOMB ART
Some of the greatest art was made for the tombs of kings and nobles. On this wooden funerary stela, a priestess raises her hands in adoration of Ra-Horakhty the falcon-headed sun god.

METALWORK
There are many paintings of craft workshops. In this detail, two jewelers finish a pectoral (pendant) and place it in a casket. To the right, a man engraves an inscription, while another is working on a golden sphinx. Other scenes in the same tomb show controllers weighing gold and checking finished articles. In reality, this workshop must have been noisy, dirty, and very hot.

BOAT-BUILDING

EGYPT'S HIGHWAY was the Nile. Everything from grain and cattle to coffins and building stone was transported by water. Only the best boats were wooden, because wood was very rare. Most travelers and fishermen punted through the shallows on rafts made from bundles of reeds.

ADZE

Blade

STEERING OAR
The Egyptians steered their boats with special oars mounted on the stern (back). This brightly painted example was found in a boat pit near the pyramid of the pharaoh Senusret III (c.1850 B.C.). The Eye of Horus was a symbol of protection.

String

Bow

BOW DRILL

Drill bit

WOODWORKING TOOL
A carpenter's tools have changed little since ancient Egyptian times. Saws, chisels, and axes have all been found. This adze was used for hacking and planing, while the bow drill bored holes for pegging pieces of wood together.

Man uses adze to smooth hull

CARPENTERS AT WORK
Boat-building is an ancient craft. This tomb scene from Saqqara dates from about 2300 B.C. The Egyptians had not yet discovered iron, and all tools and pegs were made of copper and wood.

Sun canopy

Attendant

Mummy

Oars

MODEL BOAT
Egyptians put model boats in tombs in the belief that the boat would carry the dead person's mummy to the afterlife.

Prow carved to look like a bundle of papyrus

Five pairs of oars

Priest

Steersman

Royal cabin

Stern

Steering oars

KHUFU'S BOAT
The best preserved boat is the funeral barge of King Khufu. It was found in 1954 in a sealed pit next to his tomb, the Great Pyramid at Giza. Made from 651 pieces of cedar, the boat is 143 ft (43.5 m) long.

NILE SAILBOAT

SEA-GOING SHIP

SAILING
Large sails were used to travel upriver against the current. Going downriver, the sail was dropped and the boat was rowed.

CARGO BOAT

WEAPONS OF WAR

THE ARMIES of the Old and Middle Kingdoms were small, and citizens were often called up to fight. In the New Kingdom, a more professional, permanent army was established, with corps of infantry, scouts, and marines. Chariots held two soldiers; one handled the horses and the other fired arrows at the enemy.

LONG SWORD

SHORT SWORD

DAGGER

GODDESS OF WAR
War goddess Sekhmet has a lion's head and a woman's body. She was said to stand by the pharaoh in battle, armed with arrows "with which she pierces hearts."

BLADES
Daggers with tapered copper blades were carried in wooden sheaths. Swords (first short, then long) were introduced during the New Kingdom.

FIGHTING FORMATION
Foot soldiers trained to fight in strict formatio moving together and presenting the enemy with a wall of shields. These soldiers wear kilts and carry spears.

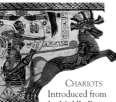

ARROWHEADS

For thousands of years arrowheads were made from stone (especially flint), bone, or the hardwood ebony. Bronze was not used until c.1800 B.C.

FLINT HEADS

BRONZE HEADS

CHARIOTS

Introduced from the Middle East in .1650 B.C., chariots revolutionized warfare. Here, Tutankhamun res arrows at Nubian enemies om the raised platform of is chariot.

ARCHER

Massed units of archers led the assault. On foot or riding in chariots, they showered the enemy with arrows. Many archers came from Nubia, which Egyptians called "the Land of the Bow."

SILVER-SHAFTED AX

CEREMONIAL AX

AXES

Battle-axes were used all across the Middle East. The ceremonial ax was probably awarded to a warrior for bravery.

ARCHER'S AID

An archer wore this guard on the wrist of his bow hand to protect himself from the lash of the bowstring.

SOLDIER ON HORSE

The army relied on charioteers rather than on a cavalry. This rare picture is from the Greek era.

MERCENARIES

The Egyptians supplemented their own forces by relying on foreign mercenaries, who were allowed to retain their own weapons and costumes.

BATTLE AX

THE PYRAMIDS

ALREADY ANCIENT by Tutankhamun's
times, the Pyramids of Giza have awed
people ever since they were built – more
than 4,500 years ago. Pyramids are tombs
made to house the mummies of kings.
Their massive size and the precision
of their construction are amazing.

▲ TRUE PYRAMID
▲ BENT PYRAMID
▲ STEP PYRAMID

ALL THE PYRAMIDS
The biggest and best-
preserved pyramids are
the three at Giza. There
are more than 80 others
in Egypt – mostly ruins,
all but buried by shifting
desert sands. The first
pyramids had stepped or
bent sides. Then came
the classic (true) shape.

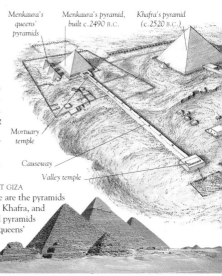

Menkaura's queens' pyramids

Menkaura's pyramid, built c.2490 B.C.

Khafra's pyramid (c.2520 B.C.)

Mortuary temple

Causeway

Valley temple

THE THREE PYRAMIDS AT GIZA
From left to right, these are the pyramids
of pharaohs Menkaura, Khafra, and
Khufu. The three small pyramids
in the foreground are "queens'
pyramids." The wives
and the children of
King Menkaura are
probably buried here.

• The Pyramids of Giza are one of the seven wonders of the ancient world and the only one still standing.

• The four sides of the Great Pyramid are aligned exactly with true north, south, east, and west.

• A dream told Thutmose IV to free the Sphinx from the sands that buried it.

HE SPHINX

his massive stone figure of a lion with the head of a king ouches before the pyramid complex at Giza. The Sphinx's ce is believed to be a likeness of pharaoh Khafra.

Great Pyramid, built by King Khufu c.2550 B.C.

Tombs of nobles and officials

Covered causeway linking Khufu's valley temple with mortuary temple

Cultivated land

Sphinx

Nile

GIZA COMPLEX

The dead pharaoh's mummy arrived by boat along the Nile. Mourners carried the coffin up a long causeway to the mortuary temple. Here, priests performed sacred rites before laying the dead king to rest in the prepared burial chamber, either beneath or deep inside the pyramid.

Canal linked to Nile

How were pyramids built?

Egyptologists estimate that it took 100,000 men 20 years to build the Great Pyramid at Giza. But how was it built? The most popular theory is that workers slid the massive blocks of stone up ramps onto the pyramid. Since little real evidence exists, we will probably never know for sure.

SQUARING OFF
One tomb painting shows masons using chisels and mallets to smooth down blocks of stone.

RAMPS OR LIFTING MACHINES?
An ancient Greek traveler wrote that workers had used lifting machines to raise stones. But he was told this 2,000 years after the pyramids were built. Ramps are less work and so more likely.

Four times many men

WERE THE PYRAMIDS BUILT LIKE THIS?
This model illustrates how the Egyptians may have built the pyramids. Workers unload the stone blocks from boats, then slide them up a long ramp to the top of the pyramid.

Mud-brick ramp is built higher as pyramid grows

Stacks of stone blocks

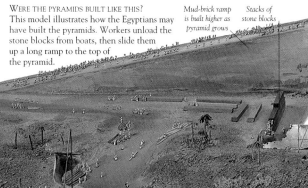

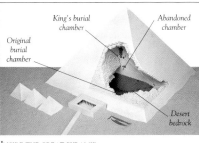

King's burial chamber

Abandoned chamber

Original burial chamber

Desert bedrock

INSIDE THE GREAT PYRAMID
A complex network of passages and dead-end chambers lies within Khufu's pyramid. Workers sealed the shaft leading to the burial chamber with huge blocks of stone.

BUILDING STONES
The pyramid core was made from local limestone. The outer layer – mostly gone now – was high-quality limestone brought by boat from Tura on the east side of the Nile, south of Giza.

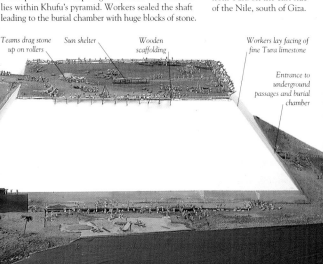

Teams drag stone up on rollers

Sun shelter

Wooden scaffolding

Workers lay facing of fine Tura limestone

Entrance to underground passages and burial chamber

TEMPLES

EGYPTIAN TEMPLES were awesome structures with massive stone walls and rows of columns carved with hieroglyphs and religious images. A temple was the home of a god. Ordinary people could only enter the outer court. In dark rooms at the temple's heart, priests performed sacred rituals.

TEMPLE OF LUXOR
Ramses the Great enlarged this temple and added two obelisks and six colossal statues.

KING-SIZE SCULPTURE
Sculptors used wooden scaffolding to carve the towering statues of kings. Only the pharaoh could be shown as large as the gods in temple statues.

SON OF THE SUN GOD
The pharaoh was believed to be the son of sun god Amun. This "Birth Room" at Luxor Temple has a series of carvings that illustrate Amenhotep III's divine birth.

Elevated roof

Papyrus-shaped columns

Pictures of gods

COLOSSI OF MEMNON
These giant figures are all that is left of the temple of Amenhotep III, the biggest ever built. A stela records that it was "inlaid with gold throughout, its floors paved with silver."

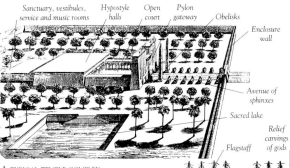

Sanctuary, vestibules, service and music rooms

Hypostyle halls

Open court

Pylon gateway

Obelisks

Enclosure wall

Avenue of sphinxes

Sacred lake

A TYPICAL TEMPLE COMPLEX
The temple was part of a huge complex with farms, workshops, Houses of Life (offices), and Houses of the Book (libraries). Each temple owned great tracts of land, where food was grown to be offered to the gods.

Flagstaff

Relief carvings of gods

PYLON GATEWAY
People entered the temple through a pylon gateway, which was often flanked with seated statues and obelisks. High above, on wooden flagstaffs, flew the gods' flags.

Hall contained 134 columns

HYPOSTYLE HALL AT KARNAK TEMPLE
This powerful temple owned land all over Egypt, and its priests virtually ruled the country at several periods. This is a reconstruction of Karnak's Great Hypostyle Hall. A temple symbolized the creation of the world, which is why the hall's cluster of columns were shaped like plants.

CRAFTS

IN LARGE WORKSHOPS, skilled craftsmen made pots, carved wood to make mummy cases and furniture, cured hides to produce leather, and worked metal and glass to make jewelry and everyday items such as magic amulets, tools, bowls, and even early drainpipes.

Glazed with bright pattern

STRIPED GLASS VESSEL
Glassy materials were made before the pharaohs. But glass was not mass-produced until c.1400 B.C. The glass was not blown, so vessels were uneven

Wadjet eyes
Lotus flower
Birds

GOLD PECTORAL
The finest jewelry was made in royal workshops. This gold pectoral – a large pendant worn on the chest – is inlaid with gemstones and colored glass.

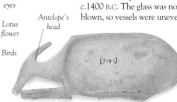
Antelope's head

IVORY ANTELOPE
From predynastic times, the Egyptians used ivory from elephants and hippos to carve a variety of everyday objects. These carvings were often shaped to fit the cylindrical shape of the tusk or tooth. This skillfully crafted toilet dish was made in about 1300 B.C.

POTTERY WORKSHOP
By Old Kingdom times, pots were being made on potters' wheels. After a few days drying in the sun, pots were smoothed and then fired in kilns.

FORMING LIP OF CUP

SHAPING OUTER SURFACE

CUTTING CUP FROM CLAY BASE

STARTING A NEW CUP

GOLD HAWK

Metals were smelted over an open fire. Before the New Kingdom, when bellows were invented, rows of men stoked the fire by blowing down pipes. The liquid metal was poured into a mold, cooled, and beaten into shape. Dipping in liquid gold was one way to gild objects.

Feather detail

Hollow for mummy

CAT MUMMY CASE

Carpenters made items for both homes and tombs. Because of the shortage of wood, these craftsmen excelled at joining small pieces together by dovetailing. Wooden dowels hold the cat's mummy within this case.

Carved wood

Dented and worn

WOODEN MALLET

TOOLS OF THE TRADE

A carpenter's main tools were wooden mallets, flint scrapers, and bronze-bladed axes, saws, adzes, chisels, and bow drills.

Nut top

PIERCERS

Animal hides were cured with the mineral alum. Then saddlers used piercers and knives to make leather sandals, ropes, and bags.

PATTING DUNG   STOKING DUNG-BURNING KILN   CUPS ARE PLACED IN KILN   FIRED CUPS ARE CARRIED AWAY

EGYPTIAN ART

THE BEAUTIFUL ART of ancient Egypt was produced by teams of anonymous painters and sculptors. They worked in tombs, temples, palaces, and houses. Their art is highly stylized; figures are almost always depicted in formal poses, and it is difficult to recognize individuals because most subjects are given perfect features.

Artists used grids to calculate "divine proportions"

GRIDLINES
Artists began by drawing a grid. Then they sketched in figures and objects, scaled up from examples in pattern books. Master designers checked and made corrections before work began.

PERIOD STYLES
Each period had its own distinctive artistic style. The art of the Amarna period is dramatically different. This statue of King Akhenaten has the heavy hips and long, oddly distorted face that are typical of the time.

IN A PAINTER'S WORKSHOP
Painters worked on wooden panels or straight onto statues or walls. They applied the paint in flat blocks of color, with no shading or gradations of tone.

SOME CHARACTERISTICS OF EGYPTIAN ART
Artists portrayed everything in its most recognizable
form. For example, the human body was shown in
profile, but the eyes and chest were face forward.
Hieroglyphs were like a caption to the picture.

SKETCHING
Artists worked out
ideas with scale
models or rough
sketches on ostraca
(fragments of stone
or broken pottery).

ART FACTS
• Tools and paints were
so precious that foremen
issued them each
morning and locked
them away at night.
• Fragments of a
gigantic statue were
found at Tanis. The big
toe is the size of a man.

MUMMY CASE
The imagery of
religious art had
deep meaning to
the Egyptians.
The gods and
symbols painted
on mummy cases
and tombs were
to help the dead
avoid the dangers
of the underworld.

9 5

Sculpture and carvings

Ancient Egypt was rich in stone, and
sculpture was the most important artform.
Copper or bronze tools were used to carve
softer materials like limestone and fine
woods. These could then be coated with a
plaster mixture called *gesso* and painted in
bright colors. Hard stone, such as granite,
was carved with pounders made of stone.

*Ready for
crown*

Metal was cast
or else beaten
into shape.

RAISED RELIEF
This is an example of
raised relief, in which
the background is cut
away to leave the figures
raised above the surface.

SUNK RELIEF
In sunk relief, the outlines of the
figures are first gouged out. Then the
details within each figure are modeled
at various depths. This is a sunk relief
of Pharaoh Thutmose III (c.1450 B.C.).

*Drawn
guidelines*

THE FACE OF QUEEN NEFERTITI
Unfinished statues give us many clues about the
way sculptors worked. This half-finished bust,
marked with guidelines, was found in the ruins
of a workshop in the abandoned city of Amarna.

TWO HEADS OF KING USERKAF

Each stone has its own qualities, making it suitable for certain purposes. Here are two heads of the same king. The colossal one is carved in granite, the smaller one in schist.

Pink-speckled Aswan granite

LOST WAX METHOD

This bronze figure of King Thutmose IV was made by the lost wax method. The figure was modeled in beeswax. This was then coated in clay and heated until the wax melted. Finally, liquid metal was poured into the clay mold.

Eyes are set in copper

LOOKING LIFELIKE

Some statues have inset eyes. This man's eyes are made from calcite with brown obsidian irises. The effect is so lifelike that the eyes seem to follow you around a room. This is the head of the seated scribe, shown on page 22.

GRANITE PHARAOH

Kings' statues were usually carved from hard stone, since they were made to last. This 3,500-year-old granite statue of King Sobkemsaf proves they did.

RELIGION

WORSHIP AND BELIEFS 100
MYTHS AND LEGENDS 102
THE SUN GODS 104
GODS AND GODDESSES 106
MAGIC AND POPULAR RELIGION 108
PRIESTS AND RITUALS 110
DEATH AND BURIAL 112
PREPARING A MUMMY 114
JOURNEY TO THE AFTERLIFE 116
MUMMY CASES 118
VALLEY OF THE KINGS 122

WORSHIP AND BELIEFS

LIKE OTHER ANCIENT PEOPLE, Egyptians believed that all events were controlled by the gods. By wearing amulets (lucky charms) and giving offerings to the gods, the Egyptians hoped for a happy life. They also hoped that the gods would help them live on after death.

PROTECTED BY THE GODS
This mummy case is covered in images of gods and magic symbols meant to help the dead person in the afterlife. A Greek wrote that Egyptians were "religious beyond measure, more than any other nation."

ANIMAL GODS
Many gods were thought to live on earth inside animals. This ram-headed sphinx represents the god Amun.

Spell for the soul of t dead perso

Tomb

Mummy is made ready for the tomb

REPRESENTING THE PHARAOH
The gods were kept happy by priests, who made offerings and conducted rituals in the name of the pharaoh, the sun god's representative on earth. Here, priests perform rights to help the dead person achieve eternal life.

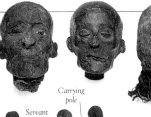

THREE MUMMIFIED HEADS
To live forever, Egyptians had to have their bodies, especially their faces, preserved in a life-like way. The spirit of a dead person could thereby recognize its body when it returned to the tomb.

Carrying pole

Servant with fan

CARRIED AWAY
A rich man was buried with this model of a sedan chair carried by three porters. He expected them to come to life after his tomb was sealed.

FACTS ABOUT RELIGION
• The sacred Apis Bull was treated like a god, kept in a luxurious part of the temple, fed the best food, and buried like a pharaoh when it died.
• Many Egyptians were buried with 365 shabti figures – one to help on each day of the year.

VIEW OF HEAVEN
In the ideal world shown on his funerary stela, Iy smells flowers with his family. The stela would keep his name alive as he lived these scenes in the afterlife.

MYTHS AND LEGENDS

THE EGYPTIAN CREATION STORY has many versions – most begin in an ocean of chaos. There were hundreds of other myths and legends. But because everyone knew the stories, they were never written down, and few have survived. Luckily, the story of god-king Osiris and his victory over death was recorded by a Greek writer.

IN THE BEGINNING

One creation myth tells of a time when Nun, the eternal ocean, filled the universe. When the waters subsided a primeval hill appeared, on which stood the creator god – the sun god Atum.

ATUM

Isis nurses the infant Horus, her son by Osiris

THE GODS ARE CREATED

Atum's children, Shu (air) and Tefnut (moisture) created Geb (earth) and Nut (sky). At first Geb and Nut were joined, but Shu came between them – so separating heaven and earth. Geb and Nut had four children – Osiris, Seth, Isis, and Nephthys.

ISIS AND HORUS

Osiris became king and took sister Isis as his queen. Jealous brother Seth killed Osiris and cut up the body. Isis collected the pieces and made them into the first mummy. Osiris lived on as god of the underworld.

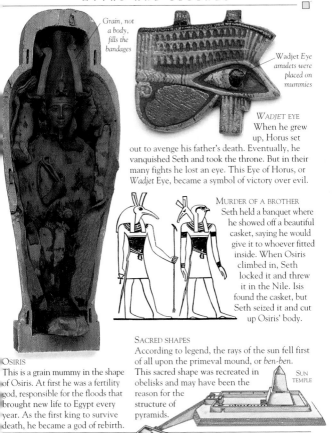

Grain, not a body, fills the bandages

Wadjet Eye amulets were placed on mummies

WADJET EYE

When he grew up, Horus set out to avenge his father's death. Eventually, he vanquished Seth and took the throne. But in their many fights he lost an eye. This Eye of Horus, or Wadjet Eye, became a symbol of victory over evil.

MURDER OF A BROTHER

Seth held a banquet where he showed off a beautiful casket, saying he would give it to whoever fitted inside. When Osiris climbed in, Seth locked it and threw it in the Nile. Isis found the casket, but Seth seized it and cut up Osiris' body.

SACRED SHAPES

According to legend, the rays of the sun fell first of all upon the primeval mound, or ben-ben. This sacred shape was recreated in obelisks and may have been the reason for the structure of pyramids.

SUN TEMPLE

OSIRIS

This is a grain mummy in the shape of Osiris. At first he was a fertility god, responsible for the floods that brought new life to Egypt every year. As the first king to survive death, he became a god of rebirth.

THE SUN GODS

SOURCE OF ALL HEAT AND LIGHT, the sun was worshipped from earliest times. This life-giving force took many forms, each represented by a different god or personality. The rising sun was a scarab beetle; at noon it was Ra, the orange disk itself; while in the evening it took the form of a ram. Satirical literary texts depict the setting sun as a dribbling, decrepit old man.

AMUN-RA
During the New Kingdom, power moved to Thebes in the south. Theban priests merged their local god Amun, a creator god, with the powerful sun god Ra. Throughout the land, Egyptians worshipped Amun-Ra as chief god.

Akhenaten and his family worship Aten

AKHENATEN, THE SUN KING
To break the power of the Theban priesthood, King Amenhotep IV banned all gods but Aten, the sun in its purest form. It was depicted as a disk with rays that touched with human hands. The king changed his name to Akhenaten and built a new city dedicated to Aten at Amarna.

WINGED SCARAB
The scarab is a
beetle that rolls up
balls of dung to lay its eggs
inside. Egyptians believed that a giant
scarab made the sun in the same way and then
rolled it over the horizon and across the sky.

*Scarab god
clasps the sun
in its claws*

*Prayers to
the sun
god*

SAILING THROUGH THE NIGHT
When the sun set in the West,
the Egyptians believed it sailed
through the underworld on a boat
before rising again in the East.
Here, the god Nun steers the boat
safely through the waters of chaos.

IMHOTEP
The cult of the sun
began at Heliopolis.
Here, King Djoser's
chief minister Imhotep
designed the first
pyramid – possibly as
a stairway, so the dead
pharaoh could join
the sun god in the sky.

SUN STRUCK
Heliopolis means "Sun
City." In its temple, priests
kept a triangular stone, the
ben-ben – believed to be
the first object struck by
the sun's rays when the
world was created. This
tomb cap is carved in
the same magical shape.

RA-HARAKHTY
Sun gods are
usually depicted
with the disk of the
sun on their heads.
The god on the far
right is Ra-Harakhty,
a falcon-headed sun
god and a version of
the sky god Horus.

GODS AND GODDESSES

EGYPTIANS HAD A DIZZYING number of gods – one ancient text lists 740. But only a small number were worshipped in the same place at the same time. All the forces of nature were represented by gods or goddesses. Temples were dedicated to state gods or important local deities and controlled by an elite priesthood. Ordinary people were excluded.

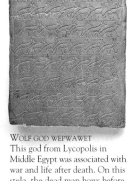

Ptah is depicted with a tight skull cap pulled over his shaven head

Flail

PTAH
The cult center of this god was Memphis, capital city during the Old Kingdom. By New Kingdom times Ptah had become a state god. He is always shown as a man, wrapped up like a mummy. He was a creator god and a patron of craftsmen.

WOLF GOD WEPWAWET
This god from Lycopolis in Middle Egypt was associated with war and life after death. On this stela, the dead man bows before Wepwawet in the hope that the god will help him live forever.

MIN
The fertility god Min wears two tall plumes on his hat and holds a flail – an agricultural tool. One of his symbols was lettuce, which the Egyptians considered a fertility food.

MAAT

The basic laws of the universe – justice, truth, and order – were represented by the goddess Maat. Her name meant "just." She wore the *Feather of Truth* on her head. Maat is often shown held by the god Ra as a symbol of justice.

Palette and pen

HATHOR

Some gods had different roles in different parts of Egypt. Hathor, goddess of love, music, and dance, was shown as a woman or a cow. She was also associated with the sky and held the sun between her horns. In Thebes she was a protector of the dead.

KHNUM

This ram-headed creator god is sometimes shown molding people on a potter's wheel. At Aswan, Khnum was guardian of the Nile and worshipped as "he who brought the flood."

THOTH

Many gods were associated with animals. For example, Thoth, the god of writing and wisdom, was depicted as an ibis – a bird that the Egyptians thought was wise. Here he is shown as an ibis-headed man writing with a scribe's pen and palette.

BASTET

Worship of the cat goddess Bastet began at Bubastis, in the Delta. In later times she became popular all over Egypt, and her annual festival was a national celebration.

MAGIC AND POPULAR RELIGION

THE STATE GODS played little part in normal life. If they had a sick child or a son at war, Egyptians asked protection from more down-to-earth gods. People wore amulets (lucky charms) and recited prayers and spells to ward off disease or disaster.

Taweret was shown as a pregnant goddess

OFFERING SHRINE

Like most ancient people, the Egyptians tried to please the gods by giving offerings of food and drink. They did this at temples, in chapels set up next to tombs, or in small shrines inside the home.

Lotus-bud shape

BES

Part dwarf and part lion, Bes was a popular household god. He carried a knife and a musical instrument, whose sweet sounds warded off bad spirits

TAWERET

Childbirth was dangerous. Egyptians prayed and put their faith in Taweret, the goddess of childbirth. She had a hippo's body, a lion's feet, and a crocodile's long tail.

MAGIC WAND

This magical stick was made from a hippo tusk. It is carved with powerful symbols, and it could be used to create a defensive barrier around a part of the house. These wands were also used to protect a child or a sick person.

HOUSE CHARM
This stela asks god Horus to protect the family from the dangers of daily life. He tramples on two crocodiles and grips snakes, lions, and scorpions in his hands. Above Horus' head, Bes pokes his tongue out at evil spirits. Magic spells cover the stela's sides.

MEDICAL TOOLS
Egyptians believed in magic, but they were also highly skilled at medicine. This temple carving shows a range of medical instruments, including forceps. One papyrus lists over 700 prescriptions for different ailments, grouped according to the sick organ.

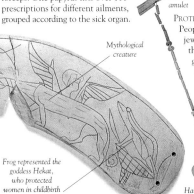

Broken amulet

Thoth as a baboon

PROTECTIVE NECKLACE
People wore amulets in their jewelry. This necklace has the goddess Taweret, the gods Horus and Thoth, and a lion to defend the wearer from any harm. Similar amulets were tucked in the wrappings of mummies.

Mythological creature

Frog represented the goddess Hekat, who protected women in childbirth

Hawk-headed Horus

Taweret

A lion for defense

PRIESTS AND RITUALS

ANCIENT EGYPTIAN PRIESTS were called "servants of the gods." Their job was not to preach to the people, but to keep the gods happy and fulfilled. They did this by performing elaborate rituals in the sacred inner sanctums of temples, where only senior priests and the pharaoh were allowed to enter.

Cup for burning incense

Hair in sidelock of youth

Offering table

PURE ONE
To show their purity, priests shaved their heads and bodies and washed many times a day. This man burns incense and sprinkles water from the sacred lake. In the inner sanctum of the temple, the priest chanted "I am a Pure One" as he approached the gold statue of the god.

Bucket held water from sacred lake

CHILD PRIEST
There were many different classes of priests. This one wears his hair in a sidelock of youth, not because of his age, but to show that he is acting as the loving son of the god.

SITULA (SACRED BUCKET)

INCENSE BURNER
As incense burns, it lets off a mild, sweet-smelling smoke. It was used to purify temples and to please the gods that lived in them. The handle of this incense burner is shaped like the sky god Horus.

Holder for incense

Sacred tool

Hawk head

Leopard skin

RITUAL TOOL
Here, King Ay holds a sacred tool to perform the Opening of the Mouth ceremony on the mummy of Tutankhamun. He wears the leopard-skin robe of a priest.

Eye of Horus

51067

Priest worships goddess Mut

Leg of meat

MIRROR
At the heart of the temple was a gold statue of the god. The priests washed it, dressed it, and placed food before it several times a day. The god was sealed in its shrine at night, then "woken" in the morning. This is a god's vanity mirror.

Head of moon god Khons

Ivory handle

6031

FOOD OFFERINGS
This offering tray is inscribed with pictures of food. The food that the priests offered to the god was grown on the temple's large estates. In reality, the god did not touch the food – the priests ate it later on.

1 1 1

DEATH AND BURIAL

THE EGYPTIANS WANTED TO LIVE forever.
To achieve this, they believed that a dead
person's body had to be preserved, or
"mummified." The mummy was then
buried with elaborate rites and a book
of magic spells to help it in its journey
through the treacherous underworld.

Pieces of gold leaf

GIRL MUMMY
This is the body
of a girl who died
over 2,000 years
ago, aged eight
or nine. Her body
was coated in oils
and resins to stop
it from decaying
and then covered
in gold leaf – maybe
because Ra, the sun
god, was believed to
have a skin of gold.

Ba *bird*   Mummy

THE MUMMY'S SOUL
Egyptians believed that a person's spirit
took several forms. One of these was the
Ba, similar to a soul. The Ba – depicted as
a bird – left the body at death. Only when
it returned would the person live forever.

TOMB OWNERS

Statues of the dead were placed in the tomb chapel to make sure that the gods knew who was buried there. Loved ones visited the chapel to put offerings before the statues.

A HUMBLE HEAVEN

The Egyptians' idea of heaven was a rural paradise, presided over by the god Osiris. They called it the *Field of Reeds* – a place where the sun shone and people worked in the fields, planting and harvesting their crops. In fact, it was just like Egypt – except grain grew a foot taller.

Husband and wife

Head of a jackal

The dead were often shown in the doorway

ANUBIS

The god of death and embalming was the jackal-headed Anubis. He was thought to guard mummies and necropolises (burial grounds). A priest wearing an Anubis mask supervised the ritual practices that surrounded the process of embalming (preserving).

Body of a man

FALSE DOOR

Tomb walls contained false doors – gateways between the worlds of the living and the dead. The spirits of the dead were thought to come and go through these doorways.

FUNERAL PROCESSION

Mourners wailed and splashed their faces with mud, as priests dragged the mummy to the tomb. Before sealing the mummy in, the priests performed sacred rites and repeated magic spells.

PREPARING A MUMMY

TO KEEP IT FROM ROTTING away, a body was preserved by embalming. After the internal organs were removed, the corpse was washed, dried out with natural salts, and then coated with oils and resins. Finally, it was wrapped in many layers of tight linen bandages. The whole process took 70 days.

PROTECTIVE EYE
Cuts made in the flesh were covered with plates like this one. It bears a sacred symbol, the Eye of Horus, to protect the body.

RITUAL KNIVES
The internal organs were removed through an incision cut in the abdomen. The brain was drawn out with a hook passed through the nose.

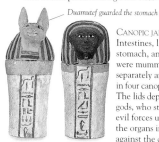

Duamutef guarded the stomach

CANOPIC JARS
Intestines, lungs, stomach, and liver were mummified separately and put in four canopic jars. The lids depicted gods, who stopped evil forces using the organs in spells against the dead.

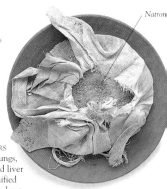

Natron

PRESERVING SALT
To stop decay, a body must be thoroughly dried out. The Egyptians did this with dry crystals of natron, a natural salt found by desert lakes. The procedure took 40 days.

KEEPING HER HAIR

This skull of a woman is 3,500 years old. Skin and flesh have rotted away, leaving nothing but hair and bone. Every hair was saved and then placed in the tomb, because a lost strand might be used in spells against her.

Braided hair

Teeth can give clues about age and diet

Linen bandages

MUMMY OF A BOY

A mummy could be wrapped in more than 20 layers of bandages. As each one was added, it was brushed with oils and resins.

WRAPPED UP

Before wrapping, the dried body was stuffed with linen and sawdust to restore shape. Sunken cheeks might be padded out and artificial eyes put in.

OPENING THE MOUTH

During mummification there were constant prayers and rituals. The most important was the *Opening of the Mouth*, held just before burial. It was meant to restore the mummy's senses.

MUMMY LABEL

Embalming was done by special priests. They made sure body parts were not mixed up by tying labels to the mummies.

JOURNEY TO THE AFTERLIFE

TO REACH HEAVEN, the Egyptians believed that a dead person had to travel through *Duat*, the underworld, where monsters and lakes of fire awaited. To fight them, the mummy was forearmed with a collection of magic spells, written in the *Book of the Dead*. The book included a map of *Duat* and many prayers to ward off evil.

BOX OF WORKERS
Shabtis are model workers placed in the tomb. They are inscribed with Chapter Six of the *Book of the Dead*.

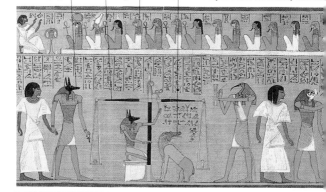

Anubis takes dead man to be judged

Scales

Jury of gods

Monster Ammit

EXTRA PROTECTION
Amulets – magic charms worn like jewelry or put into the wrappings – also helped protect a mummy from evil. The *djed* pillar was thought to give strength.

Ptah-Sokar-Osiris wearing Atef crown and false beard

Base of statue

Secret compartment

Scroll

DJED PILLAR

STILL TALKING
This tomb model of a man and woman chatting shows how Egyptians expected life to be much the same after death. They crammed their tombs with jewelry, clothes, makeup, games, food, and anything else they might need in the afterlife.

ROLLED UP
The Book of the Dead was written on scrolls of papyrus and put in the tomb. This statue of composite god Ptah-Sokar-Osiris has a hidden compartment where the scroll was kept.

Osiris, god of the underworld, presides over judgement

Goddess Nephthys with sister Isis

WEIGHING THE HEART
The final test came in the *Hall of the Two Truths*. Here, Anubis weighed the dead person's heart to see if it was heavy with sin. If it was lighter than the *Feather of Truth*, the person lived forever. If not, the heart was thrown to the monster Ammit, "Devourer of the Dead."

HEART PROTECTOR
Pectorals are amulets that were laid on the mummy's chest to guard the heart, a symbol of life. Many were inscribed with pleas like "See, this heart of mine, it weeps and pleads for mercy."

MUMMY CASES

THE FINISHED MUMMY was laid in a coffin, or mummy case. Like the tomb, this case was seen as a "house" for the dead person's spirit. Mummy cases changed gradually through the course of history, but from the earliest days the Egyptians covered them with magic symbols and pleas to the gods.

WOODEN CASE
For a long time all mummy cases were wooden. In later times many inner cases were made of cheaper materials – layers of papyrus or linen, pressed together like papier mâché.

Mummy was sealed inside while cartonnage was still wet

LACED IN TIGHT
Many mummies were buried in two or three cases – one inside the other like Russian dolls. The tight-fitting inner case was laced up at the back

Reed matting tied with twine ropes

MASKED MUMMY
This mummy of a woman is wearing a painted mask over her head and shoulders. She is also decked out in a wide selection of protective amulets.

BABY COFFIN
The earliest coffins, from about 3000 B.C., were simple reed baskets. This later example (c.1400 B.C.) contains the body of a baby. Bone deformities indicate death due to serious illness.

LOOKING GOOD
The mummy case usually presented an idealized portrait of the dead person. Analysis of this youthful-looking mummy shows that he was about 50 when he died.

FACTORY FACE
This is a wooden portrait from a coffin. Sometimes the face was made separately and pegged onto the case. These carved features were often mass produced. Regional styles allow experts to identify the area of Egypt.

SAFELY INSIDE
The priests in charge of embalming secure a mummy in its case. Wooden cases were held together with thick pegs.

WOODEN BOX
A pharaoh or an important official had an extra stone coffin, or sarcophagus. These massive structures were extremely heavy and difficult to move. This priest (Hor) had an extra wooden box instead.

Painted gods

Spells in hieroglyphs

Animal mummies

Beetles, birds, cats, crocodiles – the Egyptians mummified an amazing array of creatures. Some were beloved household pets. But most animals were mummified because of their association with particular gods. In later times, millions of animals were bred just to be mummified and buried in special cemeteries dedicated to the gods. Four million ibis mummies were found in one cemetery, each in its own pot.

Painted face

Geometric wrappings, a feature of the Roman period

CAT MUMMY
Egyptians were the first people to keep cats as pets. The earliest written mention dates from 2100 B.C. They probably tamed African wild cats, a species that was the ancestor of all modern pets. Cats were linked with goddess Bastet.

IBIS
This large wading bird is still common in the marshes by the Nile. It was sacred to Thoth, the god of writing and wisdom and patron of scribes. Biologists have used mummies and ancient pictures of ibises to show that the species has not changed in 5,000 years.

Carved falcon, symbol of the sky god Horus

Anubis, god of embalming

FOUR FALCONS
The falcon was king of the Egyptian skies and was seen as a representative of the sky god Horus. This case contains four falcon mummies and is painted with funerary scenes.

UNWRAPPED CROCODILE
Crocodiles were sacred to the water god Sobek. Priests kept pet crocodiles in luxury, feeding them on the best meat and wines.

Ears are flattened against skull

Fur

PRESERVED FISH
Other animals found as mummies include fish, vultures, owls, baboons, rats, snakes, mice, dogs, geese, scarab beetles, shrews, lizards, rams, and huge bulls.

UNDER THE LINEN
The legs of this unwrapped cat mummy have been tucked in to make a compact shape. Many of these cats were bred by priests just to be mummified and sold to worshippers visiting the temples.

Case has door at back

Each case contained a cat mummy

Tail curled up between legs

CAT CASES
These cat mummy cases all come from Bubastis, sacred city of Bastet. In later times, the festival of Bastet was an important yearly event. Huge celebrations were held in honor of the goddess, and hunting lions was forbidden.

VALLEY OF THE KINGS

DURING THE NEW KINGDOM, the capital city moved
to Thebes in the south, and pharaohs were buried in
the desolate Valley of the Kings. These royal tombs
were hidden, cut deep into the rock. Steep steps
and cramped passages led to the burial chamber,
where the pharaoh's mummy lay
surrounded by fabulous treasures.

VALLEY VIEW
The ancient Egyptians
called the Valley of the
Kings *The Great Place*.
Neighboring Valley of
the Queens was known
as *The Place of Beauty*.
This view across the
Nile shows the temple
of Queen Hatshepsut.

OVERSEER
The workers who built the
kings' tombs lived in the
nearby village of Deir el-
Medina. A few, like the
overseer Sennedjem, had
beautifully painted tombs.

*Red spots
represent
bright
stars*

*Egyptians could tell the time from
the position of constellations*

STAR-STUDDED CEILING
The Egyptians decorated tomb walls
with exquisite paintings and reliefs.
This is their view of the northern
sky at night, from Sety I's tomb.
Animals represent constellations,
which are named in hieroglyphs.

TOMB OF RAMSES IX
This pharaoh tried accused tomb robbers. One confessed "We took gold and jewels and the precious metal of his coffins. Then we found the queen and took everything that was hers and set fire to the coffins."

VALLEY TODAY
In ancient times, the valley was guarded. In spite of this, thieves had looted almost every tomb by 1000 B.C. Today, tombs in the valley are threatened by ground water, pollution, and endless crowds of tourists.

MAN AT WORK
This sketch shows a bald, unshaven mason using a chisel and mallet. Building the tombs was hot, thirsty work.

The Egyptians called this constellation Mes

Crocodile rides on hippo's back

The sun disk

Tutankhamun's tomb

In 1922, the English archaeologist Howard Carter found the tomb of a little-known pharaoh, buried 3,200 years earlier in the Valley of the Kings. Crammed inside were priceless treasures that amazed the world. As Carter said, "There were rooms full of gold, everywhere the glint of gold."

Crook and flail, symbols of the pharaoh's power

Squatting baboon gods

INNER COFFIN
The dead pharaoh was buried in three mummy cases, one inside another. The outer two shine with gold leaf, but the inner case is made from solid gold and inlaid with gemstones. This coffin weighs an incredible 245 lb (110 kg).

BURIAL CHAMBER
The outer coffin has now been returned to the stone sarcophagus in Tutankhamun's burial chamber. The walls are painted with gods and scenes from the underworld.

SHRINE DETAIL
The sarcophagus was housed in four wooden shrines, fitting one inside another. All four glittered with gold-leaf decoration.

MUMMY MASK
The most famous treasure is the portrait mask, which covered the pharaoh's head as he lay in state. He wears a falcon-headed collar, false beard, and striped *nemes* headdress. Made from solid gold inlaid with gemstones, this masterpiece weighs 22.5 lb (10.2 kg).

PAINSTAKING WORKER
Carter catalogued every detail of his work. It took him ten seasons to clear the tomb. By the time of his death, in 1939, he had published three volumes on the find.

MUMMY
The king's mummy was inside his inner coffin. In separate miniature coffins were two tiny mummies, probably his stillborn twin daughters.

THE GOLDEN THRONE
This is made of carved wood inlaid with intricate designs. The back panel shows the king and his wife.

PILED HIGH
Here, the throne can be seen as it was found. The tomb's four rooms were piled high with treasures. It had been prepared in a hurry, probably because the king died suddenly. Later the entrance was blocked by accident, so the tomb was forgotten for more than 3,000 years.

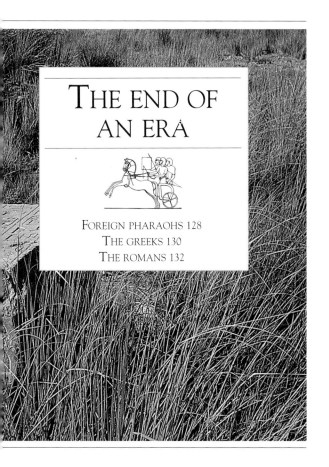

THE END OF
AN ERA

FOREIGN PHARAOHS 128
THE GREEKS 130
THE ROMANS 132

FOREIGN PHARAOHS

THE SPLENDORS of the New Kingdom ended with the death of Ramses XI in 1069 B.C. The empire was gone, and Egypt was once again split by war and chaos. In the centuries that followed, the country was invaded by its powerful neighbors. Egyptian culture still thrived, but life by the Nile was not as stable.

POWERFUL PRIESTS
The priests of Amun at Karnak Temple near Thebes became so powerful that they were able to challenge the authority of the pharaoh. This helped lead to the collapse of the New Kingdom.

TEMPLE OF AMUN AT KARNAK

CAPTIVE ENEMY
Egypt's traditional enemies came from what is now the Middle East. They included Babylonians, Hyksos, Hittites, and the Persians, who ruled Egypt twice (525–35 and 343–332 B.C.).

LIBYAN MUMMY
This is the mummy case of a Libyan called Pasenhor. Many Libyans settled in the Delta, and their chiefs ruled Egypt from 945 to 715 B.C. The Libyan pharaohs were resident kings, who wrote in Egyptian scripts and worshipped Egyptian gods.

CAT WORSHIP
The Libyan kings moved their northern capital from Tanis to Bubastis, city of cat goddess Bastet. She became one of the most popular Egyptian gods and was worshipped all over Egypt.

STRONG NEIGHBORS
For many centuries, Egypt was the only great power. But its neighbors developed and, one by one, they overran its borders. Libyan and Nubian kings lived like native Egyptians, but Assyria and Persia ruled Egypt as a colony.

NUBIAN KING
This is Taharqo, one of the Nubian kings. They ruled Egypt from 747 to 656 B.C. Their empire was bigger than Egypt at its height.

Egyptian gods

FACTS ABOUT THE ERA

• The Nubian pharaohs were buried in pyramids in the desert of Sudan.

• The Persians introduced the camel.

• According to legend, Alexander the Great was mummified and laid in a glass coffin floating in honey. It has never been found.

THE GREEKS

ALEXANDER THE GREAT conquered Egypt in 332 B.C. He built a new capital city, Alexandria, on the coast. When he died, his general Ptolemy founded a dynasty that ruled Egypt for 300 years. The new rulers spoke Greek and followed Greek law. But they respected the local culture, which continued to flourish.

TEMPLE OF ISIS AT PHILAE
The Greeks built many great temples in Egypt, dedicated to the Egyptian gods. On the walls, the Ptolemies were shown as pharaohs. But these Greek rulers rarely left Alexandria on the Mediterranean coast, and there were regular revolts against them.

ALEXANDER THE GREAT (356–323 B.C)
This great war leader was born in Macedonia, part of the Greek empire. Shortly after he became king, at age 20, he conquered the entire Persian empire, including Egypt, Syria, and Mesopotamia. His huge empire broke up after he died suddenly of a fever.

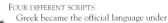

FOUR DIFFERENT SCRIPTS

Greek became the official language under the Ptolemies. Hieroglyphs were only used for religious inscriptions; priests wrote in demotic. Many documents were still written in hieratic. This detail from the Rosetta Stone shows the same text in Greek and demotic.

GREEK MUMMY MASK

The invaders adopted many local traditions. The mix of Greek and Egyptian art and religion created many new hybrids. This mummy mask has realistic Greek-style features and the headdress of a wealthy Egyptian.

Lotus flowers

Body of lion

Greek-style sculpture of an Egyptian icon

CLEOPATRA FROM TEMPLE OF HATHOR, DENDERA

ALEXANDRIA

This city became an important cultural center, famous for its lighthouse and library. The library – the greatest in the Classical World – burned down. This sphinx was part of the library complex.

CLEOPATRA VII (69–30 B.C.)

The last Ptolemaic ruler was Cleopatra VII. She tried to save Egypt from the Romans, using her legendary charm to seduce first Julius Caesar and then Mark Anthony. But, when Roman general Octavian invaded Egypt in 30 B.C., she killed herself.

THE ROMANS

EGYPT BECAME A ROMAN state after the conquest by Octavian in 30 B.C. The Roman capital was Alexandria, but the emperors ruled from Rome and took little interest in local traditions. Not surprisingly, there were regular uprisings. In A.D. 642, Egypt was invaded by Muslim armies.

AUGUSTUS (63 B.C.–A.D. 14)
Octavian, Egypt's conqueror, became Emperor Augustus Caesar. He made Egypt the granary of Rome, forcing the country to export huge quantities of wheat to feed the rest of the Roman empire.

Real rings

MUMMY CASE
Mummification of the dead continued under the Romans. Some mummy cases show the dead person dressed in their best clothes. This Roman woman is wearing a colorful toga, sandals, and wig. Her jewelry even includes real gold rings.

PORTRAIT
During Roman times a portrait, painted on a wooden panel, was often put over the face of the dead person and secured by bandages. Painted from life, this portrait may have hung in the house until the sitter died.

GOLD PARTS
Shaped pieces of gold leaf were placed over tongues, eyes, and other body parts of Roman mummies in the belief that these would restore the various functions in the afterlife.

Gold tongue to allow mummy to speak

Bunch of flowers

MUMMY MASK
This Roman mummy mask is probably one of many made in a factory from an original model. Typical of the period, he is holding a candle and a bunch of flowers, which are both symbols of rebirth.

HADRIAN (A.D. 76–138)
The only emperor to take much interest in Egypt, Hadrian was fascinated by its culture. He brought these statues back to grace his villa near Rome. He also founded a new city, named Antinoopolis, at the spot by the Nile where his lover drowned.

This area of the villa was inspired by Canopus, an Egyptian town

Pair of ducks *Crocodile* *Songbird on water plant* *Ibis*

NILE SCENE
Alexandria was a center of art. Workshops there produced many frescoes and mosaics, which were exported all over the Roman empire. This Nile-scene mosaic comes from a villa in Pompeii, Italy.

REFERENCE
SECTION

MAPS OF EGYPT 136
THE DYNASTIES 140
FAMOUS PHARAOHS 142
GODS OF ANCIENT EGYPT 146
HIEROGLYPHS 148
ARCHITECTURE 150
MUSEUMS 152

MAPS OF EGYPT

MOST OF Egypt's monuments are easily accessible from Cairo in the north and Luxor in the south. Temples are generally on the east bank of the Nile. Tombs are on the west. The pyramids of Old Kingdom pharaohs are south of Cairo, and the rock-cut tombs of the New Kingdom lie across the river from Luxor.

Rosetta
Damietta
Alexandria
Buto
Sais
Busiris
Tanis
Qantir
Merimda
Athribis
Bubastis
GIZA
Heliopolis
Abusir
Cairo
Maadi
Saqqara
Helwan
MEMPHIS
Dahshur
Lisht
Medinet el-Fayum
Tarkhan
Hawara
Meidum
Ahnas
Lahun
(Heracleopolis)
Hiba
Bahnasa
(Oxyrhynchus)
Beni Hasan
Antinopolis
Ashmunein
Bersha
(Hermopolis)
Amarna
Meir
Mostagedda
Asyut
Badari
Qaw
Akhmim
Abydos
Dendera
Amra
Qena
Nag Hammadi
Hu
Qift
(Coptos)
Naqada
Luxor
Armant
(Thebes)
Gebelein
Elkab
Hieraconpolis
Esna
Edfu
Silsila
Kom Ombo
Aswan
Elephantine
Philae

N

0   100 miles
0   100 km

PYRAMIDS OF GIZA
The three most famous pyramids at Giza, now a suburb of Cairo, are part of a large complex that includes the Sphinx, seven "queens' pyramids," ruins of several temples, and many nobles' tombs. Two earlier pyramids lie at Zawyat el-Aryan.

Great Pyramid (Khufu)
West Field
East Field
Khafra
Great Sphinx
Menkaura
ZAWYAT EL-ARYAN PYRAMIDS
Khaba

1 3 6

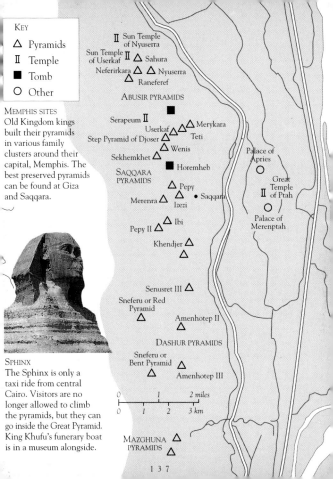

KEY

△ Pyramids
Ⅱ Temple
■ Tomb
○ Other

MEMPHIS SITES
Old Kingdom kings built their pyramids in various family clusters around their capital, Memphis. The best preserved pyramids can be found at Giza and Saqqara.

Ⅱ Sun Temple of Nyuserra

Sun Temple of Userkaf Ⅱ △ Sahura

Neferirkara △ △ Nyuserra

Raneferef

ABUSIR PYRAMIDS

■

Serapeum Ⅱ

Userkaf △ △ Merykara

Step Pyramid of Djoser △ △ Teti

Sekhemkhet △ △ Wenis

Palace of Apries ○

Horemheb ■

SAQQARA PYRAMIDS

Great Temple of Ptah Ⅱ ○

△ Pepy

Merenra △ • Saqqara

Izezi

Palace of Merenptah ○

Pepy II △ △ Ibi

Khendjer △

Senusret III △

Sneferu or Red Pyramid △

Amenhotep II △

DASHUR PYRAMIDS

Sneferu or Bent Pyramid △

Amenhotep III △

SPHINX
The Sphinx is only a taxi ride from central Cairo. Visitors are no longer allowed to climb the pyramids, but they can go inside the Great Pyramid. King Khufu's funerary boat is in a museum alongside.

0   1   2 miles
0   1   2   3 km

MAZGHUNA PYRAMIDS △

△

1 3 7

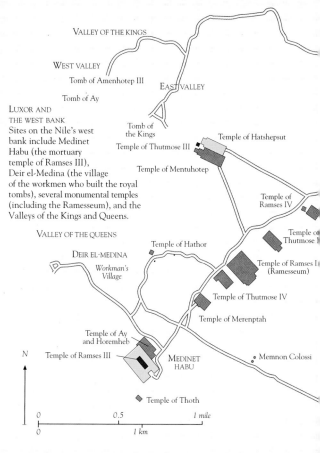

VALLEY OF THE KINGS

WEST VALLEY

EAST VALLEY

Tomb of Amenhotep III

Tomb of Ay

Tomb of
the Kings

Temple of Hatshepsut

Temple of Thutmose III

Temple of Mentuhotep

LUXOR AND
THE WEST BANK
Sites on the Nile's west
bank include Medinet
Habu (the mortuary
temple of Ramses III),
Deir el-Medina (the village
of the workmen who built the royal
tombs), several monumental temples
(including the Ramesseum), and the
Valleys of the Kings and Queens.

Temple of
Ramses IV

Temple of
Thutmose II

VALLEY OF THE QUEENS

DEIR EL-MEDINA

Workman's
Village

Temple of Hathor

Temple of Ramses II
(Ramesseum)

Temple of Thutmose IV

Temple of Merenptah

Temple of Ay
and Horemheb

Temple of Ramses III

MEDINET
HABU

Memnon Colossi

N

◆ Temple of Thoth

0   0.5   1 mile

0   1 km

VALLEY OF THE KINGS

The many rock-cut tombs in this desolate valley include those of Tutankhamun (whose mummy has been returned to his burial chamber), Ramses VI (which has brightly painted walls), and Sety I (one of the deepest).

Temple of Sety I

COLOSSI OF MEMNON

A short ferry trip across the Nile from Luxor takes visitors to the West Bank. One of the first sights is almost all that remains of Amenhotep III's mortuary temple – the massive Colossi of Memnon.

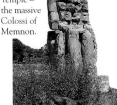

THE WEST BANK SITES

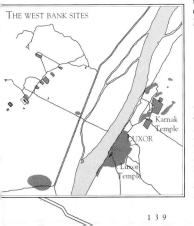

Karnak Temple

LUXOR

Luxor Temple

LUXOR

This modern city lies near the site of Thebes, the New Kingdom capital. In ancient times, the great temples of Karnak and Luxor were linked by an avenue of ram-headed sphinxes. Luxor Museum has a fine collection of antiquities.

KINGDOMS AND DYNASTIES

THE PHARAOHS ruled Egypt for more than 3,000 years. Historians usually divide this vast stretch of time into 31 dynasties. All the dates given in these tables are approximate.

DJOSER

EARLY DYNASTIC PERIOD
3100–2613 B.C.
FIRST DYNASTY
(3100–2690 B.C.)
Narmer
Aha
Djer
Djet
Den
Anedjib
Semerkhet
Qaa

SECOND DYNASTY
(2890–2686 B.C.)
Hotepsekhemwy
Nebra
Nynetjer
Peribsen
Khasekhem

OLD KINGDOM
2686–2160 B.C.
THIRD DYNASTY
(2686–2613 B.C.)
Sanakht
Djoser
Sekhemkhet
Khaba
Huni

FOURTH DYNASTY
(2613–2494 B.C.)
Sneferu
Khufu (Cheops)
Djedefra
Khafra (Chephren)
Menkaura (Mycerinus)
Shepseskaf

FIFTH DYNASTY
(2494–2345 B.C.)
Userkaf
Sahura
Neferirkara
Shepseskara
Neferefra
Nyuserra
Menkauhor
Djedkara
Unas

SIXTH DYNASTY
(2345–2181 B.C.)
Teti
Userkara
Pepy I
Merenra
Pepy II

SEVENTH/EIGHTH DYNASTIES
(2181–2125 B.C.)

FIRST INTERMEDIATE PERIOD
2160–2040 B.C.
NINTH DYNASTY
(2160–2130 B.C.)
TENTH DYNASTY
(2125–2025 B.C.)
Meryibra Khety
Wahkara Khety
Merykara

ELEVENTH DYNASTY (THEBES)
(2125–1985 B.C.)
Mentuhotep I
Intef I
Intef II
Intef III

MIDDLE KINGDOM
2040–1750 B.C.
ELEVENTH DYNASTY (Continued)
Mentuhotep II   2055–2004 B.C.

TWELFTH DYNASTY
(1985–1795 B.C.)
Amenemhat I   1985–1955 B.C.
Senusret I   1965–1920 B.C.
Amenemhat II   1922–1878 B.C.
Senusret II   1880–1874 B.C.
Senusret III   1874–1855 B.C.
Amenemhat III   1854–1808 B.C.
Amenemhat IV   1808–1799 B.C.
Sobekkara Sobekneferu
                1799–1795 B.C.

SECOND INTERMEDIATE PERIOD
1750–1650 B.C.
THIRTEENTH DYNASTY
(1795–1650 B.C.)
Sobekhotep III
Sobekhotep IV
Neferhotep I

FOURTEENTH DYNASTY
(1750–1650 B.C.)

FIFTEENTH DYNASTY
(1650–1550 B.C.)
Khyan
Apepi

SIXTEENTH DYNASTY
(1650–1550 B.C.)

SEVENTEENTH DYNASTY
(1650–1550 B.C.)
Intef V
Taa I
Kamose

NEW KINGDOM
1550–1086 B.C.
EIGHTEENTH DYNASTY
(1550–1295 B.C.)

Ahmose I	1550–1525 B.C.
Amenhotep I	1525–1504 B.C.
Thutmose I	1504–1492 B.C.
Thutmose II	1492–1479 B.C.
Hatshepsut	1479–1457 B.C.
Thutmose III	1479–1425 B.C.
Amenhotep II	1427–1400 B.C.
Thutmose IV	1400–1390 B.C.
Amenhotep III	1390–1352 B.C.
Amenhotep IV	
(Akhenaten)	1352–1336 B.C.
Tutankhamun	1336–1327 B.C.
Ay	1327–1323 B.C.
Horemheb	1323–1295 B.C.

NINETEENTH DYNASTY
(1295–1186 B.C.)

Ramses I	1295–1294 B.C.
Sety I	1294–1279 B.C.
Ramses II	1279–1213 B.C.
Merenptah	1213–1203 B.C.
Sety II	1200–1194 B.C.
Saptah	1194–1188 B.C.
Tausret	1188–1186 B.C.

TWENTIETH DYNASTY
(1186–1069 B.C.)

Setnakht	1186–1184 B.C.
Ramses III	1184–1153 B.C.
Ramses IV	1153–1147 B.C.
Ramses V	1147–1143 B.C.
Ramses VI	1143–1136 B.C.
Ramses VII	1136–1129 B.C.
Ramses VIII	1129–1126 B.C.
Ramses IX	1126–1108 B.C.
Ramses X	1108–1099 B.C.
Ramses XI	1099–1069 B.C.

THIRD INTERMEDIATE
PERIOD
1086–661 B.C.
TWENTY-FIRST DYNASTY
(1069–945 B.C.)

Smendes	1069–1043 B.C.
Psusennes I	1039–991 B.C.
Amenemope	993–984 B.C.
Saamun	978–959 B.C.
Psusennes II	959–945 B.C.

TWENTY-SECOND DYNASTY
(945–715 B.C.)

Sheshonq I	945–924 B.C.
Osorkon I	924–889 B.C.
Takelot I	889–874 B.C.
Osorkon II	874–850 B.C.
Takelot II	850–825 B.C.
Sheshonq III	825–773 B.C.
Pimay	773–767 B.C.
Sheshonq V	767–730 B.C.

TWENTY-THIRD DYNASTY
(818–715 B.C.)

Padibast I	818–793 B.C.
Osorkon III	777–749 B.C.

TWENTY-FOURTH DYNASTY
(727–715 B.C.)
Tefnakht

TWENTY-FIFTH DYNASTY
(NUBIAN KINGS)
(747–656 B.C.)

Piy	747–716 B.C.
Shabako	716–702 B.C.
Shabitko	702–690 B.C.
Taharqo	690–664 B.C.
Tanutamani	664–656 B.C.

LATE PERIOD
661–332 B.C.
TWENTY-SIXTH DYNASTY
(664–525 B.C.)

Psamtek I	664–610 B.C.
Nekau II	610–595 B.C.
Psamtek II	595–589 B.C.
Apries	589–570 B.C.
Amasis	570–526 B.C.
Psamtek III	526–525 B.C.

TWENTY-SEVENTH DYNASTY
(PERSIAN KINGS)
(525–404 B.C.)

Cambyses	525–522 B.C.
Darius I	522–486 B.C.
Xerxes	486–465 B.C.
Artaxerxes I	465–424 B.C.
Darius II	424–405 B.C.
Artaxerxes II	405–359 B.C.

TWENTY-EIGHTH DYNASTY
(404–399 B.C.)
Amyrtaeus   404–399 B.C.

TWENTY-NINTH DYNASTY
(399–380 B.C.)

Nepherites I	399–380 B.C.
Achoris	392–380 B.C.

THIRTIETH DYNASTY
(380–343 B.C.)

Nectanebo I	380–362 B.C.
Teos	362–360 B.C.
Nectanebo II	360–343 B.C.

THIRTY-FIRST DYNASTY
(PERSIAN KINGS)
(343–332 B.C.)

Artaxerxes III	343–338 B.C.
Arses	338–336 B.C.
Darius III	336–332 B.C.

GREEK PERIOD
332–30 B.C.

Alexander	
the Great	332–323 B.C.
Philip Arrhidaeus	323–317 B.C.
Alexander IV	317–305 B.C.
Ptolemy I	305–282 B.C.
Ptolemy II	284–246 B.C.
Ptolemy III	246–222 B.C.
Ptolemy IV	222–205 B.C.
Ptolemy V	205–180 B.C.
Ptolemy VI	180–145 B.C.
Ptolemy VII	145 B.C.
Ptolemy VIII	170–116 B.C.
Ptolemy IX	116–107 B.C.
Ptolemy X	107–88 B.C.
Ptolemy XI	80 B.C.
Ptolemy XII	80–51 B.C.
Cleopatra VII	51–30 B.C.

FAMOUS PHARAOHS

THE NAMES of more than one hundred pharaohs are known from inscriptions. But little is known about most of them. Much more is known about a few famous kings, like Ramses II, who covered temple walls with detailed accounts of his exploits. Royal mummies have also revealed many fascinating details.

DJOSER (C.2650 B.C.)

The earliest known reference to the sun god Ra is on a relief celebrating Djoser's name. This powerful king led expeditions to Sinai in search of turquoise. He built the first pyramid, the Step Pyramid at Saqqara. It has a network of underground chambers, where King Djoser was buried.

KHAFRA (CHEPHREN) (2556–2530 B.C.)

This pharaoh was the builder of the second pyramid at Giza, which is only 13 ft (4 m) shorter than Great Pyramid. Khafra succeeded Khufu and may well have been his younger brother. Khafra's pyramid is part of a complex of buildings, which includes a well-preserved valley temple, made from massive slabs of granite. The temple housed 23 life-size statues of the king. Among these was the famous seated statue of Khafra, the falcon god Horus perched on the back of his throne. Carved from diorite, it is now in Cairo Museum. The Great Sphinx, which crouches in front of the Giza complex, is thought to be a portrait of Khafra.

KHUFU (CHEOPS) (2587–2564 B.C.)

Khufu built the Great Pyramid at Giza. This monumental feat must have used nearly all of Egypt's workforce for about 20 years. Its treasures were robbed long ago. But in 1925, gilded furniture from the burial of Khufu's mother was discovered.

MENKAURA
(MYCERINUS)
(2526–2506 B.C.)
He built Giza's
third pyramid
(the smallest).
The earliest
known statue of
a king and queen is
Menkaura arm in arm
with his favorite wife.

MENTUHOTEP II (2055–2004 B.C.)
He was a Theban prince and
energetic warrior. In c.2040
B.C. he became founder of
the Middle Kingdom when
he conquered the north
and reunited Egypt.
He ruled for 51 years
and was buried in a
great rock tomb in the
cliffs at Deir el-Bahri.

SENUSRET III
(1874–1855 B.C.)
This Middle
Kingdom pharaoh
extended royal
control over
Egypt's many
nomes (districts). He also conquered
part of Nubia and developed the
chain of massive mud-brick forts
protecting Egypt's southern border.

HATSHEPSUT
(1479–1457 B.C.)
Hatshepsut was the
first woman
pharaoh. She
married her
half-brother,
Thutmose II,
and ruled
alongside him,
holding most
of the power.
When he died, her step-son Thutmose III
took the throne. But he was still a child,
so Hatshepsut ruled Egypt until her
death. She pursued peaceful policies,
building up the economy instead of
fighting her neighbors. She opened
new turquoise mines, sent a trading
expedition to Punt, and erected two
obelisks at Karnak. On the walls of her
temple at Deir el-Bahri, she had herself
portrayed as a man, with a false beard
and all the other symbols of kingship.

THUTMOSE III (1479–1425 B.C.)
After his step-mother's death, Thutmose
III became a powerful warrior king,
extending Egyptian
power deep into Asia.
He added to the great
temple to Amun at
Karnak and erected
obelisks, including
Cleopatra's Needle –
now in London.

AMENHOTEP III
(1390–1352 B.C.)

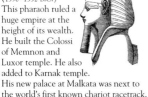

This pharaoh ruled a huge empire at the height of its wealth. He built the Colossi of Memnon and Luxor temple. He also added to Karnak temple. His new palace at Malkata was next to the world's first known chariot racetrack.

AKHENATEN (1352–1336 B.C.)

Crowned Amenhotep IV, the "heretic pharaoh" took a great interest in the sun god Aten. After six years as king, he changed his name to Akhenaten in the god's honor. His new religion was the first in history to worship a single god. He created a new city, Akhetaten, at Amarna. Here, art flourished in new, original styles, and lavish offerings were made to Aten. The pharaoh closed the traditional temples, depriving many priests of their power. He also ignored affairs of state, and the normally efficient Egyptian government was in chaos. When he died, his city was abandoned and his statues defaced. His wife Nefertiti may have ruled on alone.

TUTANKHAMUN
(1336–1327 B.C.)

The old gods were restored under Akhenaten's successor, the boy-king Tutankhamun. His father was probably Akhenaten. Another wife, Kiya, is more likely to have been his mother than Nefertiti. For most of the pharaoh's nine-year reign, power lay with an army general (Horemheb) and an elderly official (Ay). Both went on to rule Egypt after Tutankhamun died at age 18 or 19. His mummy shows skull damage, and some experts think he may have been murdered by Ay. He would barely have been remembered at all had his intact tomb full of glittering treasures not been found in 1922.

HOREMHEB (1323–1295 B.C.)

This king was a successful army general, who took the throne after the death

of Tutankhamun's elderly successor Ay. He banned the Aten religion and set about erasing the names of "heretics" Akhenaten and Tutankhamun (born Tutankh*aten*).

SETY I
(1294–1279 B.C.)
Great war leader
Sety I revived
Egypt's expansion
policy in the East
by marching into
Syria and driving
back the Hittites. In 1817, his splendid
Theban tomb was discovered. His well-
preserved mummy is in Cairo Museum.

TAHARQO
(690–664 B.C.)
The most famous
Nubian king of
Egypt, Taharqo is
mentioned in the
Bible. He revived
classic traditions
in art and followed Egyptian gods.
Ousted by Assyrian invaders, he was
buried in a pyramid in Nubia (Sudan).

RAMSES II (1279–1213 B.C.)
Known as Ramses the
Great, this king fought
an indecisive battle with
the Hittites, then signed the
world's first official peace
treaty. In the 60 peaceful
years that followed, he built many
monuments to celebrate his "victory."
Ramses II had more than 100 children.
His mummy shows that he was very tall.

RAMSES III
(1184–1153 B.C.)
He saved Egypt
from a series of
foreign invasions
and fought against
corruption. Court
members, including one of his wives,
tried to poison him. They were tried and
forced to kill themselves. A second plot
may have succeeded; he died a year later.

CLEOPATRA VII (51–30 B.C.)
The last Ptolemaic pharaoh
and the only one to speak
Egyptian, Cleopatra tried
to prevent
Rome from
taking over
Egypt. She
had an affair with
Roman general
Julius Caesar, and
they had a son. After Caesar's death, she
fell in love with another Roman general,
Mark Antony. They had three children
and planned to rule a mighty kingdom
together. But they were defeated by
Octavian, Antony's political rival.
Octavian pursued them to Egypt, where
Antony killed himself after receiving a
false report of Cleopatra's death. She
surrendered to Octavian. But when she
could not win him over, she committed
suicide – legend says – by clasping a
poisonous asp (cobra) to her breast.

GODS OF ANCIENT EGYPT

DIFFERENT GODS AND GODDESSES were popular at different times, and most changed their character over the centuries. Here are a few of ancient Egypt's most important deities.

KHNUM
Creator god Khnum was worshipped as a ram or a ram-headed man. He was said to mold children on a potter's wheel, then plant them in their mother's body.

GEB
One myth tells that the earth god Geb and his wife, sky goddess Nut, created the sun, which reborn each day. Geb is shown with a goose, the hieroglyph for his name

PTAH
The center of worship for this god was Memphis. The city priests maintained that Ptah was the supreme god, who created all the other gods by speaking their names.

ANUBIS
Jackal-headed Anubis was god of the dead and mummification. He watched over the mummy and supervised many funerary rites.

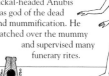

NEPHTHYS
This goddess was the sister of Isis, and she helped Isis resurrect the mutilated body of Osiris. The two sisters are usually shown together. They protected coffins and canopic jars, often in the form of a pair of hawks.

SOBEK
This crocodile god was ruler of the water, and the Nile was said to be his sweat. The main centers of worship were places where the danger of crocodile attacks was high.

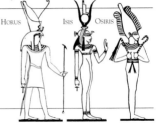

HORUS   ISIS   OSIRIS

ABYDOS TRIAD

Triads were small families of gods worshipped in a particular area. The family consisted of a husband, wife, and son. The Abydos triad was Osiris, his wife Isis, and their son, the sky god Horus.

KHONS   MUT   AMUN

THEBAN TRIAD

The chief god worshipped at the temples of Karnak and Luxor was the creator god Amun. His wife Mut was a war goddess, sometimes shown as a vulture or a lioness. Their son was Khons, a moon god, often depicted as a mummy.

FORMS OF MAAT

Many gods took various forms in different times or settings. Here are three representations of the goddess Maat, who stood for justice, truth, and order. In each of these forms, she is wearing the *Feather of Truth* on her head.

HATHOR

This goddess of the sky and of love was associated with the cow. She was often shown with horns that held the sun.

THOTH

A patron of scribes and the god of wisdom and writing, Thoth was also a moon god. He was depicted as an ibis or a baboon.

HIEROGLYPHS

EGYPTIAN picture-writing is called hieroglyphs, which means "sacred symbols" in Greek. The symbols could have various meanings.

Symbol is used for these sounds

The alphabet

Every word was written exactly as it was pronounced, although only in consonants. Vowels were omitted. The alphabet consisted of 24 hieroglyphs, each representing a single sound.

Owl faces right, so read right to left

This is a weak consonant, not a vowel

READING THE RIGHT WAY
A hieroglyphic text could be read from left to right, right to left, or top to bottom. The symbols of animals or people tell you which way to read – always read toward the faces.

W MOON UNDER WICK QUAIL CHICK	TH THREE COW'S BELLY	Y,I YOUNG INK KITE REED LEAF
J JUNK GIN SNAKE	T LOAF OF BREAD	B LEG
G GAP POT STAND	P MAT	TH THAT UNKNOWN
N WATER	D HAND	M OWL
F,V HORNED VIPER	K HILL	H TWISTED FLAX
H REED HUT	L,R MOUTH	MAY ARM ARM
A,E,O VULTURE	Z DOOR BOLT	CHIP CH TETHERING ROPE
S FOLDED CLOTH	SH POND	K BASKET

GROUP SIGNS

To save time, many hieroglyphs represent not one, but two or even three sounds together. For example, instead of spelling "sa" with two hieroglyphs, one for each of the separate sounds, it could be spelt with one symbol, a duck.

DUCK
= S+A = SA

HOUSE
= P+R = PER

BEETLE
= KH+P+R= KHEPER

TABLE WITH BREAD
= H+T+P = HOTEP

ARRANGING SYMBOLS

Symbols that made up a word did not have to be in a line; they could be fitted together in several ways, to please the eye.

TWO WAYS TO WRITE "QUEEN"

DETERMINATIVES

Some symbols are like clues. These are determinatives. They were added to the text to make the meaning clear, but they were not read as sounds.

PERSON   WALK, RUN   SEE   PLURAL

CLUE

Here is an example of a determinative. A scribe's pallete had two meanings. Next to a figure of a man it read "scribe," but next to a roll of papyrus it meant "to write."

FIGHTING EVIL

Egyptians thought symbols had power for good or evil. Scribes sometimes cut the heads off snakes or drew hawks with no claws to protect themselves from any harm.

GOOD LUCK
Symbols like the *Wadjet* Eye were thrown in for good luck.

EGYPTIAN NUMERALS

1 STROKE	**I**
10 CATTLE HOBBLE	**∩**
100 COIL OF ROPE	
1,000 LOTUS PLANT	
10,000 FINGER	
100,000 TADPOLE	
1,000,000 GOD SUPPORTING SKY	

The Egyptian counting system was based on the number 10, with different symbols for 1, 10, 100, etc. Adding up the symbols gives the total.

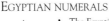

(9)

(27)

(1,200)

(54,700)

ARCHITECTURE

THE SURVIVING buildings of
ancient Egypt are mostly
religious, either temples
or tombs. Their
forms symbolize
natural cycles
and beliefs.

COLONNADE
Long colonnades were a
feature of many temples.
This one with palm-tree
capitals is from Philae.

ARTISTIC LICENSE
Some of the highly elaborate
architectural forms depicted
in tomb paintings were
obviously exaggerated.

PLANT FORMS
These Old Kingdom
columns are shaped like
papyrus stems (left)
and a palm tree (right).

CARVED
Square pillars were
sculpted with figures
of gods and men, some
massive, in relief or
even in the round.
This is the god Osiris.

Opening
bud

Decorated
with images
of gods

CAPITAL
FROM THE
TEMPLE
OF ESNA

COLUMN
Temple columns could be
fluted or smooth. But
most were sculpted, often
with elaborate reliefs that
were then painted.

HIGH GATEWAY (MEDINET HABU)
Ramses III's mortuary temple and palace are enclosed within massive, 33 ft (10 m) thick walls. This ruined gateway was the main entrance to this Theban complex.

Window

KING'S HAREM
Some of rooms in the three-story gateway were used as a harem. Walls show scenes of Ramses III being attended by young women.

Detail from the painted pavement at Akhenaten's palace

FLOOR FRESCOES
The walls and floors of palaces and villas were plastered and painted with bright frescoes of patterns or nature scenes. These are from Akhenaten's palace.

AKHENATEN'S PALACE AT AMARNA
Nothing but ruined foundations of this palace remain. But it can be imagined from paintings in the tomb of high priest Meryre. This reconstructed storage area was just a small part of the vast palace complex, which was set among landscaped gardens with many trees and shady pools.

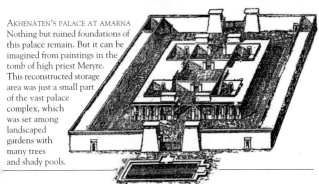

MUSEUMS

THE FOLLOWING is only a partial list of museums where ancient Egyptian artifacts can be seen. Many more exist throughout the world.

UNITED STATES

Boston Museum of Fine Arts
465 Huntington Avenue
Boston, MA 02115
The best collection in the Americas

The Brooklyn Museum
200 Eastern Parkway
Brooklyn, NY 11238

Carnegie Museum of Natural History
4400 Forbes Avenue
Pittsburgh, PA 15213

Cleveland Museum of Art
11150 East Boulevard
Cleveland, OH 44106

Field Museum of Natural History
Roosevelt Road at Lake Shore Drive
Chicago, IL 60605

Los Angeles County Museum of Art
5905 Wiltshire Blvd.
Los Angeles, CA 90036

Metropolitan Museum of Art
1000 Fifth Avenue
New York, NY 10028

Oriental Institute Museum
1155 East 58th Street
Chicago, IL 60637

The Phoebe Hearst Museum of Anthropology
University of California
Berkeley, CA 94720

The University of Pennsylvania Museum of Archaeology & Anthropology
33rd and Spruce Streets
Philadelphia, PA 19104

The Walters Art Gallery
600 N. Charles Street
Baltimore, MD 21201

Yale University Art Gallery
1111 Chapel Street
New Haven, CT 06520

AUSTRALIA

Australian Museum
Sydney

National Gallery of Victoria
Melbourne

Nicholson Museum of Antiquities
Sydney

AUSTRIA

Kunsthistorisches Museum
Vienna

BELGIUM

Musées Royaux d'Art et d'Histoire
Brussels

CANADA

Redpath Museum
859 Sherbrooke St. West
Montreal H3A 2K6

Royal Ontario Museum
100 Queen's Park
Toronto, ON M5S 2C6

CZECH REPUBLIC

Náprstkovo Museum
Prague

DENMARK
Nationalmuseet
Copenhagen

Ny Carlsberg Glyptothek
Copenhagen

EGYPT
Egyptian Museum
Cairo
*By far the best collection in
the world, including the
treasures of Tutankhamun*

Greco-Roman Museum
Alexandria

Luxor Museum
Luxor

FRANCE
Louvre
Paris
*One of the best collections
in Europe*

GERMANY
Ägyptisches Museum
Berlin
*Houses many artifacts from
Akhenaten's city Amarna*

Ägyptisches Museum
Leipzig

**Roemer-Pelizaeus·
Museum**
Hildesheim

ITALY
Museo Egizio
Florence

Museo Egizio
Turin
*One of the best collections
in Europe*

Museo Egizio
Vatican City, Rome

JAPAN
**University
Archaeological Museum**
Kyoto

THE NETHERLANDS
**Rijksmuseum van
Oudheden**
Leiden

RUSSIA
Pushkin Museum
Moscow

The Hermitage Museum
St. Petersburg

SUDAN
National Museum
Khartoum
*Antiquities from both
ancient Nubia and Egypt*

SWEDEN
Medelhavsmuseet
Stockholm

UNITED KINGDOM
Ashmolean Museum
Beaumont Street
Oxford OX1 2PH

British Museum
Great Russell Street
London WC1B 3DG
*The biggest and most
comprehensive collection
outside Egypt, including the
Rosetta Stone*

**Durham University
Oriental Museum**
Elvet Hill
Durham DH1 3TH

Glasgow Museum
Kelvingrove
Glasgow G3 8AG

Manchester Museum
The University of
Manchester
Oxford Road
Manchester M13 9PL

**National Museum
of Scotland**
Chambers Street
Edinburgh EH1 1JF

**Petrie Museum of
Egyptian Archaeology**
University College
London
Gower Street
London WC1E 6BT

Glossary

AMULET
A lucky charm, worn or carried to ward off evil.

ANKH
A kind of amulet, it was the symbol of life. Only gods and kings are shown holding the ankh.

BA
A person's spirit or soul, thought to live on after death. The *Ba* is often depicted as a human-headed bird.

BOOK OF THE DEAD
A collection of up to 200 spells, placed with the mummy to help the deceased reach the other world safely.

CANOPIC JARS
Four jars used to hold the embalmed stomach, liver, lungs, and intestines.

CARNELIAN
A red semiprecious gemstone.

CARTOUCHE
A hieroglyphic symbol representing an oval-shaped loop. A pharaoh's name was written inside the cartouche.

CATARACT
A stretch of rapids that interrupt the Nile's flow.

CAUSEWAY
A raised road or path.

COLOSSUS
A larger than life-size statue, usually of a king. They are often found outside temples.

DELTA
The flat area at the mouth of a river, where the mainstream splits into marshy branches.

DEMOTIC
Developed from hieratic writing, this cursive form is found on Egyptian monuments and papyri.

DYNASTY
A succession of rulers from related families. Egypt's pharaohs formed 31 dynasties.

FAIENCE
A glazed earthenware.

FALSE DOOR
A symbolic gateway carved or painted on tombs and coffins, through which a dead person's spirit was thought to pass.

HIERATIC
A form of writing adapted from hieroglyphs. It was written on papyrus using an ink and brush.

KOHL
Black eye makeup worn by Egyptian men, women, and children.

LOWER EGYPT
The northern part of Egypt around the Nile Delta.

MUMMY
When an Egyptian died, the body was turned into a mummy. To do this, it was dried, preserved, and wrapped in linen. Many mummies are now studied using modern medical techniques such as X rays and CT scans.

NATRON
A salt that occurs naturally in Egypt. It was used to purify and dry out the body when it was being mummified.

NECROPOLIS
A Greek word that means "city of the dead." It is used to describe Egyptian cemeteries.

NOME
A province of ancient Egypt – it was divided into areas to make government easier.

OBELISK
A tapering four-sided pillar made of stone.

OSTRACON
A flake of limestone or broken pottery that was used for writing or making rough sketches on.

PAPYRUS
A water reed used to make a kind of paper. It was the main writing material used in Egypt.

PECTORAL
A piece of jewelry that was worn on the chest.

PHARAOH
An Egyptian king. The word means "The Great House," the royal palace.

PUNT
A semimythical land that Egyptian texts refer to as a source for trade. Its exact location is still unclear, but it was south of Egypt, perhaps in Somalia.

PYLON
The monumental entrance wall of a temple.

PYRAMID
A huge tomb with a square base and four sloping sides, built to house a pharaoh's body when he died.

PYRAMID TEXTS
Religious writings carved on the walls inside a pyramid. They are an early version of the *Book of the Dead*, a collection of spells to help the dead pharaoh reach the next world.

RELIEF
A carved or molded sculpture that stands out from its background.

SARCOPHAGUS
A stone coffin that is either rectangular or human-shaped. The word means "flesh-eater" in Greek.

SCARAB
An Egyptian dung-beetle, symbol of rebirth.

SHABTI
From an Egyptian word meaning "to answer," this mummy-shaped figurine was placed in the tomb with a mummy. When the dead were called upon to work in the next life, they would call

their *shabtis*, who they believed would answer and do the work instead.

SPHINX
A statue in the shape of a lion with the head of a man or ram. A sphinx was a symbol of royal power.

STELA
A slab of stone (or sometimes wood) with text and pictures, set up in a tomb or temple.

UPPER EGYPT
The southern part of ancient Egypt. The main city was Thebes.

URAEUS
The royal cobra, worn by the pharaoh on his brow. It was thought to spit fire at the pharaoh's enemies.

VALLEY OF THE KINGS
A desolate valley on the west bank of the Nile near Luxor, which contains the tombs of many of the New Kingdom pharaohs.

VIZIER
The chief minister. He looked after government departments responsible for running the country and reported to the pharaoh every day.

Index

A

Abu Simbel, 24
Abydos triad, 147
afterlife, 101, 113, 116-17
Ahmose I, Pharaoh, 24
Akhenaten, Pharaoh, 24, 37, 40, 94, 104, 144, 151
Alexander the Great, 129, 130
Alexandria, 130, 131, 132, 133
alphabet, 148
Amarna, 80, 94, 96, 104, 151
Amenemhat I, Pharaoh, 22
Amenemhat III, Pharaoh, 23
Amenhotep II, Pharaoh, 69
Amenhotep III, Pharaoh, 72, 90, 139, 144
Ammit, 116, 117
amphorae, 50
amulets, 81, 100, 108, 109, 117
Amun, 90, 100, 128, 147
Amun-Ra, 104
animals, 46-7
   gods, 100, 107
   mummies, 120-1
ankh, 39
Antony, Mark, 131, 145
Anubis, 113, 116-17, 146
Apis Bull, 101

archery, 69, 85
architecture, 150-1
army, 25, 34-5, 84
art, 81, 94-7
Assyria, 129
Aswan High Dam, 12, 13
Aten, 104
Atum, 102
Ay, Pharaoh, 111, 144

B

Babylonians, 128
banquets, 50, 74-5
Bastet, 46, 107, 120, 121, 129
beer, 50
beliefs, 100-1
Bes, 57, 108, 109
Bible, 16
"black land," 12
Black Pyramid, 23
boats, 14-15, 29, 34, 53, 82-3
Book of the Dead, 116, 117
bread, 50
bricks, 54, 55, 80
Bubastis, 107, 121, 129
building:
   pyramids, 88-9
   temples, 90-91

C

Caesar, Julius, 131, 145
Cairo, 12
canopic jars, 114

Carter, Howard, 124, 125
cartonnage, 118
cartouches, 38, 64
carvings, 92, 96-7
cats, 46, 107, 120, 121, 129
cattle count, 45
Champollion, Jean-François, 17, 64-5
chariots, 25, 69, 84, 85
children, 36, 45, 70-1
civil servants, 29, 33
Cleopatra VII, Queen, 131, 145
clothing, 58-9
coffins, 22, 36, 118-19, 124-5
Colossi of Memnon, 90, 139
constellations, 122-3
cooking, 30, 54
craftsmen, 29, 32, 81, 92-3
creation story, 102
criminals, 31, 36
crocodiles, 14, 46, 121
crops, 48-9
crowns, 20, 24

D

Dahshur, 23
dance, 76-7
death, 112-13
Deir el-Bahri, 13
Deir el-Medina, 122, 138
Delta, Nile, 15

demotic script, 62, 65
Djoser, King, 21, 105, 142
doctors, 32

E
eggs, ostrich, 52
Egyptologists, 16
embalming, 113, 114-15
Eye of Horus, 82,
103, 114

F
faience, 19, 57
falcons, 120
famines, 15
farming, 29, 31, 44, 48-9
feasts, 74-5
festivals, 68
Field of Reeds, 31
fire, 56
fishing, 14, 68, 69, 72-3
flies, gold, 34
flint, 18, 85
floods, 12, 15, 44
food and drink, 50-1,
75, 111
forts, 35
frescoes, 54, 151
furniture, 56-7

G
games, 69, 70-1
Geb, 102, 146
Gingerella, 19
Giza, 12, 21, 83,
86-7, 136, 137
glass, 25, 92
gods and goddesses, 100,
102-3, 106-7, 146-7

pharaoh as living god,
29, 38-9, 41
  sun gods, 104-5
gold, 92-3, 124-5, 133
graves, sand, 18
Great Pyramid, 83, 88
Greeks, 130-1

H
Hadrian, Emperor, 133
hair, 45, 115
harems, 40, 151
harvests, 29, 31, 44, 49
Hathor, 41, 107, 147
Hatshepsut, Queen,
13, 35, 37, 122, 143
heaven, 101, 113, 116-17
Hekat, 109
Heliopolis, 105
hieratic script, 62
hieroglyphs, 17, 62,
64-5, 131, 148-9
hippos, 14, 19, 47, 73
Hittites, 128
Horemheb, Pharaoh, 144
horses, 52, 71, 85
Horus, 21, 38, 61, 81,
102-3, 105, 109,
111, 120, 147
houses, 18, 30, 54-7
hunting, 14, 40, 69, 72-3
Hyksos, 128

I
ibis, 107, 120
Imhotep, 105
incense, 33, 111
irrigation, 44, 49
Isis, 41, 102-3, 147

J
jewelry, 18, 45, 60-1,
81, 92, 109

K
Kahun, 68
Karnak, 91, 128, 139
Khafra, Pharaoh, 21,
80, 86-7, 142
Khnum, 107, 146
Khons, 147
Khufu, Pharaoh, 21, 28,
83, 86-7, 89, 137, 142
kings see pharaohs
kohl, 60, 61

L
lamps, 56
legends, 102-3
leisure pursuits, 68-9
Libya, 22, 24
Libyan pharaohs, 128-9
linen, 58, 59
lions, 46, 72, 121
lost wax method, 97
Lower Egypt, 18, 20
Luxor, 90, 138, 139

M
Maat, 107, 147
magic, 108-9
makeup, 60-1
  palettes, 19, 28, 61
marriage, 37, 41, 45
marshes, 14, 15
medicine, 32, 109
Medinet Habu, 138, 151
Mediterranean Sea, 12
Meidum pyramid, 44

Memphis, 106, 137
Menes, King, 21
Menkaura, Pharaoh, 21, 86, 143
Mentuhotep II, Pharaoh, 22, 143
mercenaries, 85
metalwork, 81, 93
middle classes, 32-3
Middle East, 24
Middle Kingdom, 22-3
Min, 69, 106
mirrors, 61, 111
models, tomb, 14, 31, 34, 80, 83, 116, 117
mud bricks, 54, 55, 80
mummies, 13, 101
  animal, 120-1
  burial, 112-13
  cases, 22, 93, 95, 100, 118-19, 124-5, 132
  embalming, 114-15
  masks, 125, 131, 133
  scanning, 17
music, 29, 68, 74, 76-7
Muslims, 12, 132
Mut, 147
myths, 102-3

N
Nakhte, 33
Napoleon, Emperor, 17
Narmer, King, 21
natron, 114
navy, 34, 35
Nefertiti, Queen, 37, 96
nemes headcloth, 38, 39
Nephthys, 102, 146
New Kingdom, 24-5, 128

Nile, River, 14-15
  boats, 14-15, 53, 82
  floods, 12, 44
  god of, 38
Nubia, 22, 24, 52, 85, 129
numerals, 149
Nun, 105
Nut, 102

O
obelisks, 103
Octavian (Augustus), 131, 132, 145
officials, 29, 33, 40-1
oil lamps, 56
Old Kingdom, 20-1, 22
Opening of the Mouth ceremony, 111, 115
Osiris, 23, 102-3, 113, 147

P
paintings, 94-5, 132
papyrus, 15, 62
peasants, 30-1
pectorals, 81, 92, 117
pens, 63
Pepy II, Pharaoh, 39
Persia, 128, 129
pharaohs, 38-41
  army, 34
  cartouches, 38
  dynasties, 140-1
  famous pharaohs, 142-5
  living gods, 29, 38-9, 41
  Old Kingdom, 20
  symbols, 39
pottery, 19, 57, 92-3
Predynastic period, 18

priestesses, 33, 36
priests, 33, 90, 100, 106, 110-11
Ptah, 106, 146
Ptah-Sokar-Osiris, 117
Ptolemies, 130-1
Punt, 16, 35, 52, 53
pylon gateway, 91
pyramids, 86-9
  Black Pyramid, 23
  building, 44, 88-9
  Memphis, 137
  Pyramids of Giza, 12, 21, 86, 87, 136
  robbers, 23
  Step Pyramid, 21, 105
Pyramid texts, 22

Q
queens, 41

R
Ra, 21, 104, 112
Ra-Harakhty, 105
Ramses II, Pharaoh, 24, 28, 90, 145
Ramses III, Pharaoh, 40, 71, 80, 138, 145, 151
Ramses IV, Pharaoh, 29
Ramses VI, Pharaoh, 139
Ramses IX, Pharaoh, 123
Ramses XI, Pharaoh, 128
"red land," 12
religion:
  Aten, 24
  beliefs, 100-1
  death and burial, 112-13
  gods and goddesses, 106-7, 146-7

heaven, 116-17
  popular religion, 108-9
  sun gods, 104-5
  rituals, 110-11
robbers, tomb, 23, 123
Romans, 131, 132-3
Rosetta Stone, 64-5, 131

S
Sahara Desert, 12
Saqqara, 21, 82, 137
sarcophagus, 119, 124
scarab beetles, 104, 105
schools, 62-3
scribes, 28, 33, 35,
  45, 62-3
sculpture, 96-7
Sed festival, 39
Sekhmet, 84
senet, 46, 71
Sennedjem, 25, 122
Sennefer, 41
Senusret I, Pharaoh, 22
Senusret II, Pharaoh, 64
Senusret III, Pharaoh,
  82, 143
servants, 28, 30-1, 33
Seth, 102-3
Sety I, Pharaoh, 122,
  139, 145
shabti figures, 31,
  101, 116
shadufs, 44
shrines, 108, 124
Shu, 102
slaves, 30, 31
Sneferu, Pharaoh, 20, 44
Sobek, 46, 121, 146
Sobkemsaf, King, 97

soldiers, 34-5, 84
Sphinx, 12, 87, 137
statues, 20, 22, 24, 90,
  96-7, 111, 113
stelae, 101, 109
Suez Canal, 13
sun gods, 104-5

T
Taharqo, Pharaoh,
  129, 145
Tanis, 95, 129
Taweret, 108, 109
Tefnut, 102
temples, 90-1
  Abu Simbel, 24
  architecture, 150-1
  food offerings, 51, 111
  Greek temples, 130
  Karnak Temple, 91,
    128, 139
  Luxor Temple, 90, 139
  priests, 110
  statues, 90
Theban triad, 147
Thebes, 41, 104, 122, 139
Thoth, 107, 109, 120, 147
throw sticks, 69
Thutmose III, Pharaoh,
  24, 41, 72, 96, 143
Thutmose IV, Pharaoh,
  87, 97
tombs, 28
  decorations, 13
  models, 14, 31, 34, 80,
    83, 116, 117
  rock-cut tombs, 25
  statues, 113
  Tutankhamun's,

  124-5 139
  Valley of the Kings,
    122-3
  see also pyramids
tools, 80, 82, 93
trade, 52-3
Tutankhamun, Pharaoh,
  25, 39, 40, 57, 70,
  85, 111, 144
  tomb of, 124-5, 139

U
underworld, 22, 105
Upper Egypt, 18, 20
Userkaf, King, 97

V
Valley of the Kings,
  24, 25, 28, 122-3,
  124, 138-9
Valley of the Queens,
  25, 122, 138
villages, 18, 55
viziers, 33, 58

W
Wadjet Eye, 103, 149
wands, magic, 108
weapons, 84-5
Wepwawet, 106
wigs, 58, 60
wine, 31, 50
women, 36-7
worship, 100-1
writing, 17, 62-5,
  131, 148-9

Y
Young, Thomas, 65

Acknowledgments

Dorling Kindersley would like to thank:
Hilary Bird for the index; Sarah Ponder
for design assistance; Suzanne Melia and
Kristin Ward for editorial assistance;
Caroline Brooke for editorial research;
Caroline Potts for picture research
assistance; James Anderson and Yak El-
Droubie for cartography; The British
Museum for supplying references for the
Dynasties, pages 140/141 and to The
Metropolitan Museum of Art, New York
for supplying references for the hieroglyphs,
pages 148/149.

Photographs by:
Peter Anderson, Geoff Brightling,
Christi Graham, Peter Hayman,
Alan Hills, Dave King, Nick Nicholls,
Kim Sayer, Ivor Kerslake, Karl Shone.

Illustrations by:
Peter Anderson, Russell Barnett,
Stephen Conlin, Peter Dennis,
Dave Donkin, Simone End, Eugene Fleury,
Will Giles, Thomas Keenes, Sandra Pond,
Sarah Ponder, Peter Visscher,
J.G. Wilkinson, John Woodcock.

Picture Credits
t top; *c* center; *a* above, *b* below; *l* left; *r* right.

The Publisher would like to thank the
following for their kind permission to
reproduce their photographs:

Ashmolean Museum, Oxford 45cra,cr,crb,
60tr;/The Griffith Institute 125tl,ca,cr;
Bolton Museum (jacket), 2br, 3tr, 14br,
25tr, 29tl, 30b, 88/9, 101br, 107tr, 113cr,
119c; Bridgeman Art Library 63br,
74/5br;/Louvre, Paris 56bl;/The British
Museum 68cr; The British Library/
Laurence Pordes 16cr; The British Museum
1c, 2tl, tr,bl, 3l,br, 5t, 7br, 13r, 14bl, 15cb,
16b, 17tl,cl, 18tr,c,bl, 19b, 22tr, 22/23b, 23br
29tc, 31tl,tr,cr, 32tr,b, 33tl,c,br, 34cl,clb,
36bl, 37br,tc, 39bc,tl, 40/41tc, 46/47b,
46tl,cr, 47tr,c,tl, 48/49bl, 49tl,(jacket),
51bc, 52br, 56cr, 57c, 58bl, 59r,c,cl, 60cb,
bl,tl, 61tl,r,bl,bc, 62br, 63tl, 64/5c, 70tl,
c,br, 71tr,cla,br, 73t, 76tl,bl, 77tl,c,br,
80cr, 81br,bl, 82c, 83t,ca,(jacket), •
84c,cl,cr,(jacket), 85tr,bl,crb,cr, 93tr, 94tl,
95br, 96tr, 97cl,c, 98/99, 100bl,r, 101tl,
103l,tr,(jacket), 104tl, 105tr, 106tr, 107bc,
(jacket),br,tc,cl, 109tr, 110/11tc, 110bl,br,
111bl, 112l, 114tl,cl,br,bl, 115tl,cr,bc,br,tr,
116tr,b, 117cr, 118tr,bl,cl, 119b,tl, 120cl,
121tl,ca,tr,bl, 128/9b, 129tl,tr, 131tl, 132l,cr,bc
Cairo Museum 20bl,br; Lester Cheeseman
24cr, 131r; Peter Clayton 57br, 125bc;
Robert Harding Picture Library 102bl;
Michael Holford 102cl, 105c; The Manchester
Museum 19tl,tc,tr, 24bl, 31b, 37cr,tl,(jacket)
55tr, 56bc, 57tl,tr, 68/69bc, 69cr, 80tl,cl,bl,
81ca,(jacket), 84tl, 92tr,(jacket),cl,cr, 93cl,
cr,br, 101cl,(jacket), 102tr, 105tc, 106bl,bc,
108tr,cra,bl, 108/109bc, 109br, 111br, 112cr
113tl, 117tl,tr,br, 118br, 120br,l, 131c, 133tl
tr; Metropolitan Museum of Art, New York
90/91bc; John G. Ross 10/11l, 14tr, 15tl, 16tr
20c, 21tc,br, 22cl, 23tl, 25b, 28tl, 29r,
35tr,br, 37bc, 38br, 39cl, 40br, 41cla,br, 45b
66/7, 74br, 85tl, 90c,tr, 94br, 95c, 96bl, cr,
97br,tr, 104br, 111tr, 112/3b, 122cr, 123tl,tr,c
122/3b, 124l,cr,b, 125tr, 126/7, 130bl;/Raph
34cr, 38clb; The Science Museum 53br;
Lin White 12tr,cr, 13tl, 25tl, 38tl, 39r, 41bc
78/79, 90bl, 105br, 109tl, 113tr, 122cl, 128c
130cr, 131bl, 133bl, 139tr,cr.

Every effort has been made to trace the copyright
holders and we apologize in advance for any
unintentional omissions. We would be pleased
to insert the appropriate acknowledgment
in any subsequent edition of this publication.